YOU ARE MORE THAN A NAME

Harshit Nayyar

notionpress.com

INDIA • SINGAPORE • MALAYSIA

ISBN
Paperback 979-8-89673-367-6
Hardcase 979-8-89777-357-2

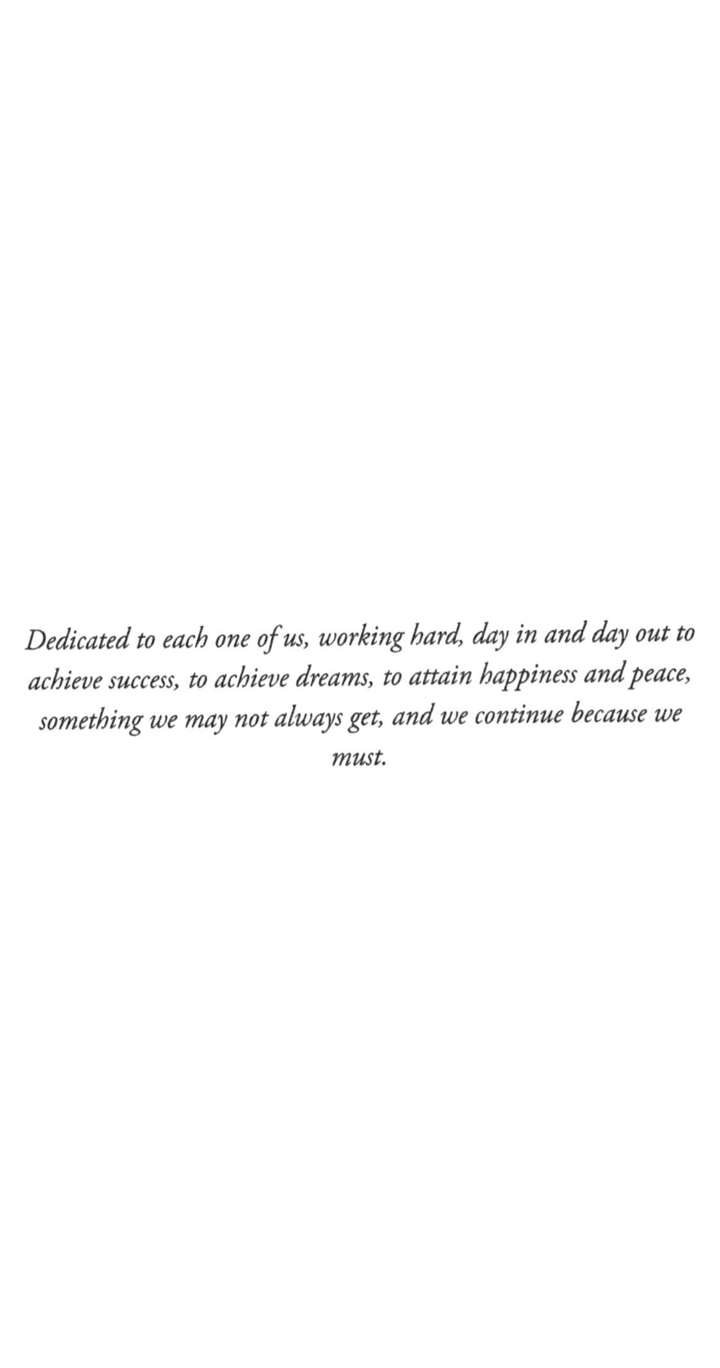

Dedicated to each one of us, working hard, day in and day out to achieve success, to achieve dreams, to attain happiness and peace, something we may not always get, and we continue because we must.

Contents

❖ Contents ❖

Acknowledgments

Thank you to everyone who has contributed toward bringing this book to where it is. You all know who you are, and I remain grateful to you.

A big "thank you" to you, the reader, as well for deciding to invest money and, more importantly, time into the book. Hope it is worth more than the rupee and the time spent.

1

How did It Begin?

Tick tock, tick tock! The sound of shoes cracking against the marble floor grew louder as Prashant approached the door of the well-furnished meeting room. Only the noise from the air conditioner coming through the vent disturbed the uneasy peace in the room.

Well dressed in a suit, albeit without a tie, nearing his forties yet looking younger because of his personality, and having his signature smile, Prashant opened the door.

The person in the room got up, a bit hesitantly, in that awkward position where one is neither standing nor sitting, and wished him:

"Good morning, sir."

"What, Saahas? This is a multinational company where we respect people and there are no sirs and ma'ams. How many times should we be telling this to everyone?" Prashant responded more in a candid rather than a preachy manner.

Saahas smiled, which looked more like a smirk. Not willing to give away too much, he calmly agreed:

"Yes, sir… err, Prashant."

"So how are you? And how is everything?" The common line that can be voted as the most used, monotonous yet effective line for ice-breaking.

"Well, everything is fine. I'm looking forward to the discussion with you."

"So, when did you reach and how has the stay been thus far?"

Wondering about the reason behind the question since he was the one who had arranged the flight and hotel bookings.

"The Delhi flight arrived late last evening, took a nap of 6 hours, woke up in the morning, and reached the office."

"Any issues so far?"

"Nothing thus far, hoping we can start soon," Saahas was getting a bit anxious now.

"Yes, sure, we will do that. I request you to take this discussion very seriously, tell whatever you feel and treat it like an interview."

This time the smirk was wider on Saahas's face, kind of intentionally willing to show the other party how he felt.

"Sure, Prashant. I will treat it like an interview, the exit interview."

The silence disturbed by the voice of ACs returned. Only this time, it seemed louder. Unarguably, it was one of the better silences encountered in recent times.

"So how did it all begin?"

2

Dronacharya

The clock struck the tenth hour of the day on 4th July as we stepped onto the marble flooring of the seemingly old but definitely well-maintained administrative building of the 1,500 MW coal-based power plant of Samriddhi Power Limited in Chhattisgarh.

Outside the building, the flag of the firm, hoisted alongside and inches away from the Indian tricolor, flew in the moist wind. Flower pots were placed along four lines next to the flag poles, holding yellow bougainvillea. Water being splashed by the fountain in front of the flags made the scenery complete.

The time of the year was supposed to be the hottest part of the year in this region of the country. But water from the fountains and trees planted around the periphery of the plant made the weather outside the building pleasant.

I, Saahas Sharma, fresh out of my engineering college, entered the building with eleven others from the same college. We all had secured campus placements in this company which offered one of the best packages. It was a day of pride for us, as we began our 'Corporate Careers'.

Twelve of us entered the building, into a big hall with the reception table in front and a row of two sofa sets on the left. As we entered, we were amazed by the tidiness of the place. White marble on the floor, shining like a mirror, placed in rectangular patterns wall to wall with walls having floor-to-ceiling carpet. The right-side wall was adorned with neatly framed photos. One photo was of the company's Managing Director, Mr. Amitabh Kapoor, with the Prime Minister of the country; the other one was of all the employees standing outside the building we just entered; the third one had the company's vision and mission statement and the values that the firm stood for.

We were guided to the conference room by the lady at the reception and while we were still in awe of the tidiness, the conference room took our level of wonder one step further. The conference room had a central table with 21 seats, 10 on each side and one in the center toward the far end from where we entered. There were seats placed next to the wall as well in case additional chairs were required. The conference room was a full leather setup, with a tablet and a microphone on every seat.

Samar from HR was there to meet us. We all knew him since he had come to the campus for placements a few months ago. He had subsequently reached out to me later on to support in documentation for those who had been selected by the firm from the college.

We all were shy in directly approaching him, as we were already in awe and yet to completely absorb the magnificence of the building we had just entered. Most of us had come from a background wherein sitting in such an atmosphere was a luxury in itself. Wanting it not to look odd and to overcome a bit of our nervousness, Samar smiled at all of us. We smiled and nodded at him.

While we were entering the conference room, we saw there were eight other similar-looking species also sitting in the room. They were also dressed in formal attire, rather seemingly fresh formals bought especially for this day. They looked at us, we looked at them and as expected, we didn't say a word to each other.

We all took our seats, and in total, there were sixteen boys and four girls, or what now seemed like sixteen men and four women seated in the room.

Samar turned towards everyone.

"Welcome, guys, to the first day, first show."

A wry smile came on his face at his attempt at humor.

"As you begin your professional journey officially, I, on behalf of the firm, welcome all Graduate Engineer Trainees, the GETs, and hope you enjoy yourselves."

"Soon the Managing Director of the firm, Mr. Amitabh Kapoor, will be here and he will be accompanied by the Director of Human Resources, Raghuvendra. They will brief you about the firm, some of which you already know and some of which you might not remember after their presentation."

While Samar, to some of us, it seems, was trying too hard to be funny, he was essentially trying to break the ice and make us feel comfortable.

"Raghuvendra, or Raghu as we all call him," Samar continued, "will also let you know about the training plan and the next steps for you."

"But before we begin, I am sure most of you don't know each other, considering you are from different colleges."

"Even those who are from the same colleges don't know each other, Sir," Kamal jumped in.

Kamal, 6 feet tall, thin-built, and having a broad face, was from the same college as me. We had interacted briefly during undergraduate studies, with our discussions being largely related to academic matters and more to the point rather than anything casual. What I had heard from some of our common friends was that he was too much into academics, was free-willed, and not someone who would always follow the line with regard to discipline. Apart from Kamal, I had also interacted with some others who were joining here but not with everyone.

"Fair point. So why don't we start," Samar remarked.

We all looked at each other, not knowing where to start.

"So, Kamal. Why don't we start with you?" Samar requested Kamal, smiling. We all laughed looking at the price Kamal had to pay for being an enthu cutlet.

Kamal began "Hi. My name is Kamal Gupta. I am an Electrical Engineer from the National Institute of Technology,

Kurukshetra. I am from Hamirpur, and I look forward to working in this company."

"Decent introduction. Thank you, Kamal."

Next up was me as I was sitting next to Kamal.

"Hi. My name is Saahas Sharma. I am a Mechanical Engineer from the National Institute of Technology, Kurukshetra as well. I have been brought up in Ranchi, Jharkhand. My interests include reading books and writing poetry. I come from a family of government professionals, having an elder brother and father both in government jobs. My mother is a housewife, sorry, homemaker, and I look forward to having a successful career in this firm."

"Now that is what you call an introduction!" Samar spoke out loudly. I was surprised to have received such a response.

"That's perfect, Saahas. Request if everyone could give their introductions on similar lines."

The introductions went around the table one by one, with all twenty of us introducing ourselves in 20 minutes.

"Thank you, everyone. I think it was good to know about everyone, including what your hobbies are. I think you can connect with each other over your hobbies if nothing else," Samar said in his now usual smiling tone.

"As it is, you folks will get a lot of time to connect in the next six months. Why, you will soon get to know as Raghuvendra will share."

"Sir," Binoy jumped in. Binoy was about 5 feet 4 inches, round-faced with slightly long hair and looked like someone who was not much into physical activities. He had, in his introduction, said he is from NIT Warangal and his interests include watching movies. His father is a businessman manufacturing air conditioners, and his mother runs an NGO.

"So, Samar sir, Mister Raghuvendra sir will be our boss going ahead." The level of respect Binoy was giving with 'Mister' and 'Sir' left only words like 'Your Highness' and 'My Lord' to show further respect. To be sure, we couldn't blame Binoy for the same, considering that we were all still conscious of our surroundings, and it was day one, or rather, hour one, of the corporate journey.

"Binoy," Samar reverted, calling out his name from the badge pinned on his shirt. All of us were given name badges for our first day so that we could be called out during our discussions with the senior management.

"First of all, there is no Mister, Miss, Sir or Ma'am in the firm. I have shared this with you earlier as well when you were supporting me with the documentation of batchmates from your college."

"And secondly, there is no boss. Only the manager whom you report to. But remember, in your career, ultimately there is one boss and that is…"

"You yourself," Rohit spoke as if to himself. But in the conference hall, it was loud enough for everyone to hear.

"Brilliant," Samar reverted. And as if on cue, everyone applauded.

Rohit sheepishly smiled. He was also around 5 and a half feet tall. In his introduction, he had mentioned that he is from NIT Warangal and that his father is a transport contractor and his mother a teacher. His interests were diary writing and going on long walks, and he always wanted to be in the energy sector considering the impact it has on the development of the countries.

"Now guys, I just got a message that Amitabh and Raghu will be here in 5 minutes. You guys can sit, make yourselves comfortable, and think about the questions for Amitabh and Raghu. And considering you have no other option, you can… wait."

Samar left the room, and there were twenty of us in the room. Clean-shaven boys, with neatly combed hair, in full-sleeved shirts, trousers, and polished shoes, having used the best deodorant affordable. Girls, with neatly washed hair, in full-sleeved shirts, trousers, and polished heels, and having applied optimum makeup.

No one, it seemed, wanted to begin with the wrong impression and thus had kept things simple and tidy.

However, we looked less like new engineers on the job, and more like fresh lambs queued up at the slaughterhouse.

No one was talking to each other and were only passing glances at each other, conscious of the fact that anyone could walk in anytime.

10 minutes later, Samar walked in followed by two men, dressed in half-sleeve shirts, khaki trousers, and formal leather shoes.

By the look of it and considering our perception of corporate professionals, they seemed to be someone junior to Samar or as the firm would like us to say, people who report to Samar. Only when Samar introduced them did our biases unshackle a bit.

"Hi friends, please meet Amitabh and Raghuvendra."

Not only our biases, but we also shook a bit that these were among the most senior personnel in the organization.

Mr. Amitabh Kapoor, the Managing Director, introduced himself, starting with his total years of experience in the industry and at the firm.

He spoke with such grace and eloquence that I lost track of what he was saying but was looking at how he was saying. It seemed like poetry in motion.

He spoke for 10 minutes about what the company's vision is, what the mission is, how many employees are there and where he wants to take the company. In between, he also asked if we knew the difference between a vision and a mission, to which Kamal said, "Not that I knew earlier but now I think we all know." This seemed to be moving to a bit of the sycophancy side, but the benefit of the doubt could be given to Kamal that at least someone spoke up. I, for some reason, was so much in awe of Amitabh that I could not speak up, but I felt I had found my next idol.

Amitabh said that vision is what you want to achieve as a company and mission is how you want to achieve that.

Amitabh ended his speech by welcoming all of us to the company and wished us successful careers with the firm.

After Amitabh's speech, Raghu came up and thanked Amitabh for his speech. He said that Amitabh's speech was always inspirational for the employees. Not that I would have disagreed with Raghu, but 'always inspirational' did seem to be on the sycophantic side. Before going into further details, Raghu tried to break the ice by asking everyone.

"Aren't you guys surprised by our dress code?"

A few among us slowly nodded.

"I am sure. Well, typically you would find people in corporate jobs wearing white shirts, black trousers, and at times a tie. If I can say so, similar to what all of you look like."

All of us laughed.

"However, when you are in a power plant, especially in a coal-based facility like ours, and you wear a white shirt and black trousers, by evening it will be difficult to differentiate between the color of the shirt and the trousers. And don't be surprised if your face looks similar."

Everyone, including Amitabh, laughed.

"So, with this dress code, you are not worried about your clothes. Not sure what to do if you worry about your face."

"As if we are here not to produce electricity but to look beautiful," Pallavi murmured under her breath. But such was the magic of the conference hall, like Rohit's, the words were loud and clear.

There was complete silence and everyone looked at Pallavi. That is when she realized that she had been louder than required.

However, Mr. Amitabh started laughing. It was followed by Raghu and Samar laughing. All three of them said in one voice.

"This is what our kids also remind us every day when we get ready!"

And everyone laughed. Pallavi's laughter was more of a relief.

Raghu then took us through the induction plan. It seemed more of an induction program rather than a plan.

"There are ten sessions lined up with the senior management of the plant today. There will be folks from different teams including Human Resources, Operations, Maintenance, Safety, Administration, Environment Control, and Risks."

"Tomorrow morning, all of us will reassemble at 10 am in this hall. After a small briefing, all of you will head to your destination for the next 6 months: Central Power Training Institute, Nagpur."

We were all fairly excited. Not with the line-up for the next 2 days, but for what followed after those 2 days: the 6-month double-paid training. Paid in one sense that the company was going to pay for it, and paid in another sense that we were going to receive our salaries for undertaking the training. We had been briefed by Samar after our recruitment on campus regarding the same. Kamal and I used to talk about this on campus, and we were excited about it.

Raghu continued.

"For the 6 months of your training, Samar will be the Single Point of Contact (SPOC) for any issues or feedback, and it goes without saying that in case he does not address your issues, you can reach out to me. My and Samar's coordinates are displayed here."

He wrote his and Samar's email addresses and phone numbers on the whiteboard of the conference hall.

"Now, I would like to thank Amitabh for taking out time to brief you, and after a quick tea, we will reassemble in this hall. Samar will take it forward from there. Good luck, folks."

We all stood up as Amitabh and Raghu left the hall. Samar asked us to enjoy some snacks and tea and coffee that were lined up in the corridor adjoining the hall through which we had entered.

That is when I saw Pallavi again. She was about 5 feet 2 inches, with curly short hair, spectacles, and someone who seemed to be into sports. She was elegant in the way she handled her food and coffee. We didn't exchange any words, and I focused more on the food. I wanted to say hi to some of the folks, but my focus on free food took over. Kamal and Binoy were chatting with each other, and it was later that I realized that such teas were not meant for free food but for something known as networking.

After 15 minutes, Samar asked us to assemble in the hall with the seating that he had rearranged.

He said that he wanted all of us to know each other better, so he had put name tags that he had, next to people from the other college. I had Rohit on my right and another person from Rohit's college on my left.

We were led through multiple sessions of half an hour each during the day by the senior management including on the company's policies, company's financials, plans for the future, safety procedures, challenges facing the industry, how some of the other power projects are coming along, and environmental considerations we need to look at in a coal-based power plant. Most of the senior management would give a 15-minute presentation and then interact with us. They asked questions and so did we.

Some of the management personnel were quite frank in giving their answers. They also gave us some insights on how we should look at our career paths and where we should invest our salaries.

All the sessions were done by 5 pm, and Samar was seated with us throughout the sessions to facilitate the interaction. For once, we thought if he did not have a better job. Later on, we realized that this was a part of his job.

Raghu came in for the last session at 5 pm and took us through the leave policies, the company's employee metrics, and plans for increasing the strength. He also shared the roles where earlier GETs are working.

I was silent for most of the sessions as it was still difficult for me to open up in front of so many people. I was speaking only when reached out to by another GET or once in a while to Samar.

After Raghu finished his session, he asked us for any questions. I finally asked my first question for the day;

"Raghu, out of all these roles that you have mentioned, which one is the most challenging?"

"Well, every role has its own challenges," Raghu quickly reverted.

"Okay, pardon me for repeating the same question in a different way. What is one way you would never like to take up?"

Everyone laughed at this version of the question, including Raghu.

"Now I need to answer this. Well, it has to be the Coal Management Plant. Not because it is one of the dustiest places but because it is also one of the most critical systems. There are so many external stakeholders with such a long lead time considering coal has to be transported from faraway places that you need to be on top of everything. If there is no coal, there is no power, at least in this plant. So, this is one role that I would like to avoid… until I can." He smiled.

We were all impressed with Raghu's insights.

"I liked this question. Even I had to think. Good."

Samar asked, "Any other questions?"

Rohit asked, "What is one thing during our GET period that we should be mindful of to prepare better for our upcoming role at this plant?"

"Another great question," Raghu said.

"Well, the most important thing is that you take each session of your training seriously. It is very easy to get distracted when you don't have someone regularly keeping a watch over you. Not just during the training period but also later in your career. You can never be sure which course would be helpful at which stage. But you should know what the key takeaways are from each session so that you can go back when required."

"Thank you, Raghu."

I actually liked how Rohit was already looking 6 months ahead to life after training, and some of us were still wondering how good the lunch was.

Binoy spoke up next.

"Sir, you talked about the different roles. Which roles will we be allotted?"

Raghu asked Samar to take this up.

"Well, it depends on multiple factors. You will be monitored during your 6-month training and after that, based on your performance and interest, you will be allotted your department. It's a long road ahead and something which you will get to know after 6 months."

After Binoy's question, there weren't any other questions.

Raghu finally said, "Okay, I think that we have had a lot of discussions during the day and must be tired. We should call it a day. It was good meeting all of you and …"

Just then, Pallavi had raised her hand.

"Yes, Pallavi," We all looked at Pallavi with a similar expression to that you have when your batchmate gets a lecture extended just when it was about to end.

"Raghu, Samar. I wanted to ask this question throughout the day but have been hesitant. Not sure if it is the right question or not."

"I am not sure what the question is, but there is nothing like a wrong question. And remember this whenever you feel underconfident before asking a question. If you ask a question which you think does not make sense, you might feel like a fool for the moment. But if you don't ask the question, you would feel like a fool for the rest of your life."

That sounded like a nice piece of advice.

"Please feel free to go ahead."

Pallavi continued, "Throughout the day in all the presentations, there wasn't a single female employee. Even today among the GETs, there are only 20% girls. What is the HR doing to correct this?"

Raghu: "Well, that sounds like a question from the investor meeting."

All of us, including Pallavi, smiled.

Raghu: "It's a great question nonetheless and something that we all, including Amitabh, have been working seriously on. The challenge is that power plants in remote locations are not considered by girls or their families to be safe places to work, and that is why these roles are not preferred. "This doesn't mean they are not safe. They are indeed safe, as you would realize over your career." Office jobs in Tier I cities are more preferred. Even during the campus hiring, when we discussed with the Campus Coordinator, we got to know that not too many girls were keen on this job. But the trends are slowly changing, and it's good to see that four of you have joined us and hopefully can set an example for others going forward."

Everyone applauded the response.

Pallavi: "Thank you, Raghu. This helps."

Raghu: "Okay. I think now, in the interest of time, we should close today's session. Let us all meet at 10 am tomorrow."

We all walked outside the hall. Cabs were waiting for us to take us to our hotels.

Most of us were tired from the sessions during the day and crashed into our respective rooms.

* * *

Next morning, all of us reached the administrative hall at 9:45 am sharp.

Before we began, Rohit came up to me and said, "Hi. I am Rohit. I really liked the way you spoke yesterday."

Not sure how to react to the compliment since I had not spoken much. But I could only say, "Thank you, Rohit. And I liked what you spoke."

Both of us smiled.

The session began at 10 am with Raghu and Samar entering the hall.

Raghu took us through the next steps of our training.

"Folks. You will be heading to Central Power Training Institute, Nagpur or CPTI as we call it, for the next 6 months. All of you will be based out of CPTI for the entire duration of the training. During the training, you are expected to attend all the courses assigned to you with utmost sincerity and dedication. While there will not be anyone from the company to monitor you, but from now on, in case you haven't realized, you are also a part of the company and this training is more or less your first Task. Management will regularly monitor your progress in the training through periodic interaction with the professors of the institute."

There was pin-drop silence after the words 'regularly monitor'.

Raghu continued, "Before you leave, we need to appoint a batch representative. Someone who can coordinate with the authorities at the institute to ensure smooth running of the training and someone with whom we can also discuss as and when required."

Pin-drop silence again. We all looked at each other. Samar asked everyone to either volunteer or put forward some names.

"Saahas," said Kamal. I was surprised to hear my name. Being from the same college and having interacted earlier, I could sense why.

"Binoy," said Rohit. Again, a similar logic seemed applicable.

Pallavi said, "Saahas." Not being from the same college and not having interacted, no logic seemed applicable.

Before some other names could be said, Raghu said.

"Okay then. Saahas will be your batch representative. Congratulations, Saahas."

I was not sure why. I was yet to digest what had happened. But there would be a lot of time for that later.

Raghu continued, "And it goes without saying that while Saahas would represent you, and you are expected to support him with proper conduct, anyone can reach out to both Samar and me anytime. Wishing everyone good luck."

With that, Raghu brought the session to a close. We all took the taxis standing outside the administrative building and headed to the railway station from where we took the train to Nagpur.

On the way on the train, there was a lot of time to think over.

I was not sure why my name was chosen.

Was it because I had interacted with Samar before? But so had Binoy.

Was it because I spoke well? So had Rohit.

Was it because life had to teach me something about being a leader? Maybe, but so does for everyone, every day.

3

Interlude - 1

Prashant: "Wait. You have mentioned details about only five people, that is Rohit, Binoy, Kamal, Pallavi and you. What about the other fifteen? You missed them."

Saahas: "If I tell in detail about them, our meeting will turn into a conference. I am not sure if we have so much time. But let me assure you, all twenty were an integral part of this journey."

Prashant (laughs): "I am sure."

He firms up and adds: "And I am very particular about getting things done on time."

Prashant continues.

Prashant: "So, Batch Representative from day one. Good start to your career. Not many people get a chance so early on. You were the leader of the group."

Saahas: "I was supposed to represent them but ended up leading them."

Prashant: "What is the difference?"

Saahas (with a smirk on his face): "Slightly huge."

4

Yudhishthira – 1

On the 7th of July, Mr. Suburaj Subrahmanyam met all of us in the large training hall of the Central Power Training Institute, Nagpur.

All twenty of us had reached Nagpur a day before and had been allotted ten rooms in Executive Hostels on twin sharing. Each room had an attached washroom, two single beds, two separate almirahs, a table, a chair, and an air cooler. We were that species which was used to residing in college hostels with a common washroom for twenty people and a fan whose revolutions you can count. For us, this was a 5-star hotel.

The roommates were randomly allocated by Samar. While Kamal had said he would prefer sharing the room with me, I got a room with Rohit. There was a common dining room downstairs, big enough for 30 people to have a meal together.

We had put our luggage in the rooms. I soon called the phone number of Mr. Suburaj that Samar had given me. He was going to be our course coordinator. He picked up on the third ring, but the conversation was not long as he seemed too busy somewhere. However, he said he was glad that all of us had reached safely and had settled in.

He asked us to rest for the day, and he would meet us at 10 am the next day in the training hall of the campus. He told me that the training hall is in the 'training block' of the campus. For a moment, I thought about mentioning that this is where the training hall should be, but decided against it for obvious reasons.

Some of us decided to take a rest while others decided to go around to explore the campus.

We all met again in the evening for dinner in the dining hall where everyone was updated regarding the plans for the next day.

"We need to assemble at 10 am in the training hall. Mr. Suburaj will meet us and he will share what lies ahead. Let us all arrive on time. Breakfast will be available from 9:15 am onwards," I said.

"Where is the training hall? And what do we need to carry?" asked Binoy.

"It is in the training block, which is a 5-minute walk from here. Right now, I don't think we need to carry anything apart from a pen, a notebook or a diary and ourselves," I responded with a smile.

Binoy also smiled back.

"Let us all reach at 10 am tomorrow. For the day after tomorrow we will see," Kamal remarked.

Mr Suburaj Subrahmanyam was standing inside the training hall when we reached the next day. The training hall was less of a hall and more of a classroom.

There was a projector attached to the ceiling with a podium at the front of the hall. Rows of tables and chairs were lined up.

We all entered the room and took our seats. As our habit was, we skipped the first row of seats. No one wanted to be the front bencher, at least on the first day.

Mr. Suburaj saw this and gave a sarcastic smile. He first looked at the front seat and then at us. We could sense what he was hinting at, so I decided to go ahead and occupy one of the first rows. I thought others would also join, but even after 30 seconds, I was the only one, and it looked embarrassing.

Without waiting any longer, Mr. Suburaj started with his introduction:

"Hi. My name is Suburaj Subrahmanyam. You can call me Subbu. I am a lecturer at this institute and will also be your course coordinator. Before I begin, let me ask, who is Saahas?"

I raised my hand.

"I should have guessed it. I was told by Samar that you are going to be the batch representative. I can see now why."

It was difficult for me to understand why he said that and if it was a compliment or something else.

Suburaj continued,

"I have been with the institute for more than 10 years, and I can assure you that you have come to one of the best places for training in the power sector in India. Here, you will interact with the technical experts in the power sector, and considering your course is structured for a period of 6 months, you will get a lot of opportunities to learn, unlearn, and relearn."

He then took us through the various modules of the course, which included a site visit to the Kaparkheda thermal plant near Nagpur and a course on the power plant simulator. He said that there would be regular evaluation of the progress during the course and that we would need to sign attendance for every session, which would be with the batch representative.

On a PowerPoint slide, he showed the names of the professors in the institute and their respective subjects. He also mentioned that there would be guest lectures throughout the 6 months and evaluation during the course, details of which he would share as we go along.

After an hour, he finished, and the professor who was going to take the topic 'Steam Generation' walked in.

The lectures for the day ended at 5 pm and were mostly introductions by the various professors in the institute regarding their courses. There was an hour's lunch break in between.

At the end of the day, Kamal, Binoy and a few others decided to go out and explore the city since it was the first time in Nagpur for most of us.

At 5:30 pm, Subbu called me to his room. He gave me a bunch of papers which had the name of each student and asked me to ensure everyone signed against their name every day for each session. He also shared a bundle of books which he asked me to share with all the students. This was going to be the course material. He said that he would rely on my support for smooth sailing and learning for everyone and would give his best to ensure a good learning experience, provided we all ensure discipline and sincerity. I assured him of utmost cooperation from our end.

Subbu's office boy and I walked back from Subbu's office to the Executive Housing. As we crossed the institute's sports ground, I saw Pallavi running on the track in the ground. She had, during her introduction at the plant earlier, mentioned that she enjoyed sports, and it was impressive to see that she was on the task from day one. She was an Electronics engineer.

I went into the room and saw Rohit sitting on the chair writing something in a small diary.

"Day 1 already started doing homework and revision, buddy. Want to top the training already?" I asked Rohit.

Rohit smiled back, "No, nothing much. Just writing some thoughts in the diary. Not much into going out or sports."

"Good. Whatever makes you happy. Even I like to stay indoors and read books."

"Oh. What kind of books?"

"Mostly non-fiction. What about you?"

"Well, I used to read. But these days I like to write."

"What do you write?"

"Whatever the pen and paper agree on." He smiled as if to convey that he was no longer interested in taking this topic forward.

I tried to change the topic and asked him what he thought about the course and the next 6 months.

He said, "It is still Day 1 and I am sure those who have designed this course are much smarter than me to comment on. Let us see how it goes, hope it should go well."

I could only nod.

Rohit and I hadn't spoken much earlier. I thought that since we would be roommates for the next 6 months, it would be better to break the ice. While I enjoyed talking, but only with those whom I knew well, Rohit seemed a bit reserved even with those he seemed to know well. However, I had noticed that whenever he spoke, there was quality in his words.

At the end of the day, before dinner, I also started writing notes in another notebook which was essentially one or two bullets for learning from the day. I remember the advice Raghu had given to us earlier and thought of giving it a try. I was not sure for how many days I would pursue this but thought of giving it a shot, there wasn't anything to lose as such and my roommate Rohit was as it is busy with his diary, so I had some inspiration. I started writing the key takeaways. I never knew what Rohit wrote. I got to know about it a few days later. I hope I hadn't got to know about it.

In the evening, some of us who didn't go out went for dinner in the dining room. Others came late, and Kamal had asked me to inform the cook not to wait for them.

After dinner, Rohit and I walked out of the dining room. We saw Pallavi sitting in the lobby of the hostel. She said hello to us and asked if we would like to go for a walk. She mentioned that she is used to undertaking long walks and it would be good if she had company.

I looked at Rohit, who nodded. We thought it would be a great idea to explore the campus. We agreed and went outside the hostel onto the roads of the campus. The campus was lush green, and the greenery was visible even under the dim light of street lamps. The bushes and grass were neatly trimmed, and the trees were properly marked.

Three of us spoke about where we were from, what our background was, and what our interests were. Most of this we had already spoken about in our introductions at the plant earlier, but it was good to have a one-on-one refresher. Pallavi did most of the talking, and Rohit the least.

We walked for 15 minutes, and the cool night breeze made it a pleasant one. Just as we were about to enter the hostel, I asked Pallavi.

"There is one question that has been going through my mind for the last few days. Not sure if I should ask you?"

"What? Why did I take your name for the batch representative?"

I was surprised.

"Yes. But how do you know?"

"Relax. I could see your expression when I took your name."

"We all could," Rohit added with a smile.

Pallavi continued, "Remember when you introduced yourself and your family? You corrected yourself when you said your mother is a homemaker and not a housewife. That showed two things. One, your thinking is not old school and secondly, the self-confidence you have that you could correct yourself in front of a large audience."

"Thanks," was all I could say.

"Don't mention it." was the response.

I just smiled and the three of us went to our rooms. Others had also by then returned from their short city tour.

The activities picked up from next week. Both inside the classroom and outside the classroom.

5
Yudhishthira - 2

Next morning all of us were in the dining room for breakfast at 9:30 am. We were done in 20 minutes and proceeded to attend the sessions for the day. Subbu was going to take the first session on 'Thermodynamics'. While most of us had studied the same during our graduation, the purpose of the session was to ensure that, considering we were from different colleges and Engineering Branches, everyone was on the same page.

As Subbu entered, I realized there was one person missing. Subbu came in and started the session. Kamal walked in 15 minutes later. It was surprising to see him late considering we had met at the breakfast table.

I glanced at him with a puzzled look, and he just smiled back. Subbu also gave Kamal a similar look but continued with his session. I circulated the attendance sheet, and everyone signed it.

During the break, I went to Kamal.

"What happened? Hope everything is fine?" I asked.

Kamal reverted, "What happened? Yes, everything is fine."

"Then why were you late?"

"I wasn't late. Everyone came in 15 minutes earlier," he said sarcastically.

I looked at him without saying anything. He continued.

"Relax, Saahas. It's just training. Fifteen minutes here, fifteen minutes there do not matter."

"It's not about 15 minutes, Kamal. It's about the discipline. It matters. And just because we could, does not mean we should," I said, slightly firmly.

Kamal did not react much, and I thought it was only wise not to take the discussions any further. We went back for the rest of the session.

During the lunch on Friday, when everyone was slightly relaxed, I decided to get a sense check on how the mood was. Because personally, I was enjoying the sessions, I felt it would be good to know what others thought. I asked everyone how they were feeling. Friday is one day when people are most relaxed and thus candid to share their opinions. Remember, if you ever want a waiver from your manager for anything, Friday is the day.

"The lectures are really good and I am liking them," said Pallavi.

"I think the presentations could be better styled," said Binoy.

"Okay. What do we mean by better styled?" I further inquired.

"I mean currently there is too much content on one slide. It becomes boring and mundane to read. There could be less content, more graphs and pictures, and a larger font. That would make the classroom sessions more interesting."

"Fair. Does anyone else have any other suggestions?"

Most of them agreed with Binoy and didn't have much to add.

So, I went to Subbu after lunch, before the sessions for the second half could begin.

"Hi, sir. Can I come in?"

"Yes, Saahas. Feel free. And it's Subbu."

"Sure, sir. I mean Subbu."

"Please tell. What brings you here?"

"Well, I had some feedback. Are you fine with it?"

"If it's a positive feedback, it is welcomed. If it is criticism, it's more than welcomed," Subbu replied in jest in his approachable nature.

"Well, it's more of the second part. If you allow."

"How much more permission do you need? Don't be hesitant. Feel completely free. Come, let us sit on the sofa, have some coffee and talk. Maybe you would be more comfortable."

"Sure. Thank you."

"Let me know when you are done with the formalities, and we can speak," he smiled.

"Ha-ha. Sorry, Subbu."

"Again?"

"Okay. First of all, the material that is being discussed with us is very good, and most of us are enjoying it."

"Thank you. That does not sound like a criticism. But still, carry on," he smiled. I continued.

"However, what people feel is that the delivery can be more interesting."

"Interesting as in? Should I ask the professors to sing a song as they speak?" We both laughed.

"Not really. But there could be other measures."

"Go on…"

"Make the content easier on the eyes. Instead of plain text or a few charts put together on slides, we could have more graphs, figures, flow charts, and diagrams with minimal text, which would be both easy to understand and discuss with the trainees."

"Fair suggestion. It's not that I haven't thought about it in the past. But there has been a challenge."

"Which is?" I asked.

"Most of the professors are experts in their fields. They traditionally know how to deliver lectures. But this presentation and all is still a relatively new thing for most of them. So not sure how to get them to make these slides. If someone helps, we could get this moving."

"Okay. I will help," I replied in the affirmative.

I shared the idea that I had thought of and discussed with Rohit while coming to meet Mr. Suburaj, who was now Subbu.

Subbu would request all the professors to share their planned slides for the coming week on the Friday of the previous week. I, along with one more person from our batch, would make the edits over the weekend and send them back to the professors. Professors could review the slides before their session and let us know in case they desire any changes.

Subbu was understanding and agreed.

Before I left the room, Subbu called me from behind and asked, "Good to see you are making this effort, but why take the pain?"

"Because it is for everyone's learning."

Subbu smiled and nodded.

At dinner, I told everyone about the plan. Everyone liked the plan; however, only for a few minutes because then there was a bigger question to be addressed.

"So, who is going to volunteer for this, apart from me?" I asked.

There was silence.

I asked Kamal if he would be part of this. He refused.

"I would be happy to be a part of this, but I have other commitments such as going to the gym and preparing for MBA coaching."

I thought about persuading him but realized he was not keen, and the reasons seemed more like excuses. My sense was that it was only going to take a few hours on the weekend which anyone could take out, only if they wanted to.

I asked again, this time trying to add some motivation.

"Anyone who wants to be part of this project which would improve the learning of our batch? In fact, not only our batch but of future batches that would come to this institute."

Again silence.

"You are the batch representative. You decide," remarked Binoy.

"This is pure volunteering. So, don't want to put it on anyone. Because ultimately you won't get anything apart from maybe some good karma points." I smiled.

Still, there was no response from anyone.

I thought of not taking this further and going all alone on this to see how things work out. If not for the amazing improvement that could have been brought about with two people, at least there would be some improvement. Plus, a commitment was made to Subbu so there was no backing off.

Next morning, before breakfast, I started working on the presentations on my laptop. Subbu had sent the draft presentations on Friday evening.

While I was working, Rohit woke up.

"Can I help?" Rohit asked.

"Sure. But why didn't you say that yesterday?" I asked.

"Because I was not sure if you would actually walk the talk. In fact, none of us thought that someone would actually make the effort. Now that you are actually doing it, it makes me feel I should also be a part of it. Trust me, if it works, others would also be a part of this."

"Trust me, if it works, there would not be a requirement for others to be a part of this," I remarked sarcastically.

Rohit agreed and joined me after breakfast. However, he asked me not to make much noise about his contributing to this considering he wanted to keep a low profile. I can only tell if someone asked.

Both of us started working on the slides on Saturday morning. On Saturday, Rohit would search the internet for the graphs and charts, and I would do the initial formatting of the slides and put the contents into bullets.

On Sunday, both of us would sit and look at the presentations to see if the revised presentations seemed simpler to read and made sense to us. By 5 pm on Sunday, we would send the presentations to Subbu.

It did take some effort, but it was interesting because we actually got a chance to read through the presentations in detail, which we might not have done otherwise. Maybe this was the 'good karma'.

Next week, the revised presentations were presented by most of the professors. By most, but not all.

I decided to again take a sense check of the mood on Friday. This time most were fine with the presentation while others felt that considering they were encountering some of the courses for the first time in their education journey, it was going over the top. But they said they would come on board with it.

Before we could finish the lunch, Kamal remarked.

"Now that this presentation thing is sorted, can we do something about the timings?"

"Sure. What do we want to do about the timings?" I asked.

"Do we need to be on time or present for every lecture? Can't we just skip some of these?"

I just smiled and thought it better not to continue with the topic. Less of a smile but more of a smirk, which meant 'No'.

After lunch, I went to Subbu.

Before I could ask Subbu anything, he asked me.

"So, how did everyone like your presentations?"

"Sorry, Subbu. Not my presentations but ours, in fact, everyone's presentations. And to answer your question, it was liked by most of the batch."

He smiled.

"Good. Even I liked the presentations. The style made even me interested in my own slides which I have been delivering over the years."

We both laughed.

"Subbu. If I may ask. Why didn't all the professors give the revised presentations? Have there been any issues?"

Subbu smiled.

"Good that you asked. Actually, it's not about you but the professors. Change is a difficult thing, buddy; you will realize it later in your career. It is difficult to change yourself, and more difficult to change others. You need to create awareness, desire, knowledge, and ability, and reinforce the changes. While we have covered most of the parts, others are still not there. So, some professors were comfortable with their own content and did not like delivering something which was made by someone else. You can call it ego, you can call it a comfort zone."

"Okay. But is there something that we could do about it? Like go and explain to them what we are trying to do."

"No. No. Don't try to stretch so far. I think you did a decent job. Keep continuing with this. Don't worry about the professors. I know them well and will handle that part."

"Okay. By the way, it wasn't only me, but Rohit also worked with me on this. In fact, without Rohit, this would not have been possible"

"Great. Congratulate Rohit as well on the good job."

"Sure, Subbu, I will." And I left the room.

* * *

Next week, the sessions went on as per schedule with most of the professors delivering the revised presentations. In some of the sessions, Kamal would come 10 minutes late. Gradually, two more folks started coming late. Everyone saw but chose not to react.

On Friday, we had a guest session by the Chairman of the institute, Mr. Gopalan, or Gopal Sir as he was called. We were three weeks into the course, and he wanted to check on our understanding and share his experiences. Subbu accompanied Mr. Gopalan.

We all sat down, and Mr. Gopalan introduced himself. He shared that he had more years of experience in the power sector than most of us had on the planet. All of us laughed. He also shared that he had spent a major part of his career in the power plant before he decided to move to academics. He shared which parts of the country he had worked in, which departments he had worked in, and which one was the most interesting. He said that he has significant on-ground knowledge, and we should ask in case of any questions.

We were not prepared to ask questions, so there was complete silence.

After 2 minutes of awkward silence, he sternly remarked, "Either you ask or I will ask."

We thought this was going to be a lecture. It was turning out to be a viva.

"There are only two instances when you don't have any questions. Either you understand everything or you don't understand everything. Hope it is the former one." He remarked.

We all laughed again. But this time the joke was on us.

Subbu started looking a bit impatient.

Mr. Gopalan continued,

"Subbu. Who is the batch representative?"

I raised my hand.

"So. No questions, young man? Should I ask, then?"

"No, sir. In fact, I had a question…"

"When you mentioned that you have had a strong on-field experience… why did you decide to shift to teaching, I mean academics?"

The question being thought, framed, and spoken at the same time.

However, there was a sense of slight relief that at least something was being asked.

"Why? Do you think there is anything wrong with being an academic?" Mr. Gopalan reverted.

The response was not expected. But I was glad that at least he had acknowledged the question.

"No, Gopal, Sir. There is nothing wrong. And I am sure that is why you have done it," I replied cheekily.

Subbu had a look of terror on his face. That is when I realized what I had done. I looked toward my right. Binoy was smiling. The realization and embarrassment doubled.

However, Mr Gopalan genuinely smiled.

"Good sense of humor."

"And to answer your question," he continued, "Working in the field does bring about a lot of learning and experiences. It throws new challenges at you every other day, which makes life more exciting. But after a point, you feel like giving back and sharing what you have learned. That brought me to academics. Even if today you ask me to go back to work in a power plant, I would happily do so, but somewhere I feel I am adding more value by being in this institute."

"Thank you, sir," I said and sat down.

"More questions, please," Subbu remarked.

"Sir, how have you been able to achieve your life goals?" asked Kamal.

"Passion, young man," remarked Mr. Gopalan. "Passion is what will change things. Every day will not be fruitful, every day will not be rewarding. There will be occasions when you would want to give up. And trust me, it is not only you who would be thinking that way; there will be others who would be facing the same situation every day and hoping for the pain to go. Ultimately, there will be two kinds of people: those who do not lose their focus and keep going with whatever they have, and those who give up for the seemingly more comfortable things. The only difference between these two people is that one does not reach the goals that they set for themselves, while the others are known as winners. The goals that were beyond their means anyway."

Everyone applauded the answer.

A couple of folks, including Binoy, asked technical questions to which Mr. Gopalan gave elaborate responses. Mr. Gopalan's session cum viva lasted an hour. Subbu thanked Mr. Gopalan for taking out his time. Mr. Gopalan said it was his pleasure and he liked the quality of the questions. Before leaving, Mr. Gopalan turned to me and said

"One more thing, young man."

"What, sir?" I asked, surprised.

He smiled and said, "Next time, be prepared with the question. Don't frame it while you speak."

"Don't think we gave him that option, Sir," Subbu candidly remarked. Everyone, including Mr. Gopalan, laughed.

Mr Gopalan and Subbu left the room.

In the evening, Rohit, Pallavi and I went for our after-dinner walk. We had started invariably going on a walk every day after dinner, thanks to Pallavi.

"Good you asked the question today," Pallavi said.

"So did others," I remarked.

"They had the time, you didn't. They had the option to ask or not, you didn't," Rohit replied.

"I believe it's part of the job of being the representative."

"No. You acted like a leader. You could have very well not asked or put in a simple 'I will ask later'. But you knew if you don't tackle the issue then, it will come on others. You acted as if it was your team and no one should get impacted."

"If you say so." And I smiled. Quite ironically, a few weeks later, I was going to repeat Similar words that Rohit said. Albeit to a different set of people.

"By the way, Mr. Leader, there is another interesting challenge coming your way," Pallavi said.

"Folks. Can we stop this leader-representative thing? "My name is Saahas." I spoke a bit agitatedly since it was getting a bit embarrassing.

"And what is this challenge, by the way?" I asked.

"Your friend from college, Kamal, does not like your 'be on time' policy."

"What is the 'be on time' policy? We are not in college anymore, we are in a professional setup and everyone needs to be disciplined."

"You understand that, we understand that, not sure everyone understands that," Pallavi reverted.

"They should, otherwise they will have to," I replied slightly sternly.

"Good luck with that," Pallavi said.

"You would need it." Rohit closed the walk for the evening.

* * *

Next week, the sessions continued as per the schedule.

Kamal started coming in 30 minutes late for the opening session. Soon more people started coming at least 10 minutes late. The end result would be that out of twenty only 10 would be seated at the scheduled time and the professors would look at empty benches and then at me. However, I allowed everyone to mark their attendance for the session. This happened in one of Subbu's sessions as well, and he passed an angry look at me without saying much. By now, I had known Subbu enough to realize what his expressions implied.

But realizing that soon it could be only one person sitting at the scheduled time, I decided to act.

On Thursday, after the morning sessions, before we broke for lunch, I went in front of the entire batch.

"Folks. I have to share something. It is being noticed that some of us are being late for the sessions. While in a one-off case it is understandable that it could be beyond one's control, a repeat of the same shows a lack of our commitment."

"Relax, buddy. Don't take it too seriously," Kamal remarked.

"Please allow me to finish, Kamal," I said softly.

"Sure," Kamal replied.

"Considering these repeated cases, it has been decided that anyone coming late for any session by more than 5 minutes will not be allowed to mark their presence. In case you are late, you must message me in advance so that I can relay it to Subbu."

"Sorry, Saahas. But I don't think you are the one who can make a decision on this policy," Binoy remarked.

"Exactly Binoy. I do not make a decision on the policy. My job is to ensure the policy is implemented effectively. Just to recall for everyone's benefit, our daily record goes to Samar in HR. I don't think anyone wants any wrong record to be shared. I hope you realize where I am coming from." I responded politely but firmly.

"In case someone has any issues with this, please talk to Subbu or Samar. Thanks." I added and closed.

We all went for lunch, and the sessions continued for the rest of the day.

"That was a bold move, Mr. Leader," Pallavi remarked during the evening walk.

I gave her an angry look.

"Sorry, Saahas. But you did act like the leader. But if it's not okay with you, I will not call you one."

"You know I was thinking about what would be the reaction of everyone. I personally never wanted to impose such a strict decision. But the challenge was that in case something goes wrong or there is indiscipline, Subbu and Raghu pick my neck. I am the one responsible."

"I hope I am not taking a risk," I added.

"Risk is when you don't know what you are doing. In this case, I think you know what you are doing," Rohit added.

"But what if…" Before I could finish, Rohit added.

"Don't worry, buddy. You do what is right. Even if you have to bear the cost of your decisions. The cost of seemingly wrong decisions would always be more than that of seemingly right decisions."

"Thanks, Rohit. This sounds reassuring."

"What costs are both of you talking about, by the way?" Pallavi jumped in.

"He will soon get to know," Rohit reverted.

"Thanks again, Rohit. This did not sound reassuring," I said. All of us laughed and went back into the hostel.

* * *

Next week everyone was on time for almost all the sessions. Kamal was late for one of the sessions by 15 minutes, yet he marked his record sheet that was being circulated. When the sheet came to me at the end, I struck out his name for the session. I did not make much noise about it, but where I was sitting, Binoy could see me striking out the name. He later relayed this to Kamal. Kamal was never late again. The issue was sorted. Only on the surface.

Activities in the training hall continued as usual. People had started taking an interest in a lot of activities outside the classroom as well. I continued taking key takeaways for each session in my diary following the habit of Rohit. Kamal had got others including Binoy to join the gym, while Pallavi would spend her evenings on the field. Pallavi had got a couple of more folks to take to running, and they had also formed a small cricket team which usually played on weekends. Pallavi asked everyone if they would want to be a part of the team. Rohit and I agreed to play on the weekends, while Kamal and Binoy were not too keen as they were busy with other engagements. Pallavi was able to put together a team of eleven players, and we did decently, winning every other match considering we were not as much into playing the game as we were into watching it. Pallavi was our star player with her swing bowling and quick running between the wickets.

6
Rohit's Diary

One Sunday when Rohit and I were done with editing the presentations for the next week, I was going through my diary when I saw Rohit's diary kept open on the table while Rohit had gone down to the dining hall for a cup of coffee. I picked up the diary out of curiosity and started reading it.

* * *

For Some Chapters Have To Be Closed

"I am leaving tomorrow morning." the Message flashed on the phone.

"What? Why? How? All of a sudden?" Normal reactions that would come into one's mind. However, even before that, for a duration of time that science is yet to define, the mind goes blank. You want to react, but you cannot react. It is the moment when you realize that something has ended inside you. Your mind regains presence, and you gather all the strength to reply. But wait, should it be a text message or a call, plain text on the screen, or words supported by voice which might give a hint regarding the person's condition? What if the message is not responded to? What if the call is not picked up? Final decision: not to do anything.

Exactly 2 minutes later, the number is dialed; so much for mental strength or rather lack of it.

"So, you are leaving. All of a sudden? What happened?" Voice trying to hide the volcano inside as much as possible.

"No, this was planned for a week back, but I just wanted to let you know now."

"Why are you telling me even now?" Volcano was getting a push.

"For we shall never meet again," the voice on the other side seemed to be trying hard to not show any expression.

"Why?" This had been the most used word either verbally or in thoughts for the past 5 minutes, but there was more to come.

"Hmm… Don't know," came the reply.

"Fine, go. Have a good life ahead. As it is when we shall never meet again why even once more." The Volcano had burst. Not sure was this spoken as an aggressive reply to a threat or as a message coming out of courage that one gets when one has realized there is nothing more to lose.

"No, it is not that we shall never meet again. But just one more time." The voice on the other side seemed to be more confused than the voice on this side.

"Okay. Let me see. I have the final exam scheduled for tomorrow. It might be difficult for us to meet." With her going away, the feeling of having already failed the biggest exam had started creeping in.

"Hmmm…"

Pause for 15 seconds and then a flip-flop. It had rained on the lava.

"Fine, I will meet you tomorrow morning at 6:30. Drop me a message when you are about to leave."

"Ah… okay." And we disconnected the phone.

Next Morning

"Bye then. Good luck with your job. Earn well and have a good life ahead."

"Yes. Without you? Sure." Left unsaid for the better.

"You too have a good life. Hope everything gets sorted and you stay happy always."

Moments of silence for what seemed like an eternity. We both were looking at each other. Uncertain about the next moment that awaits us. Certain that we knew months back that this moment would come. For she did not know how to end it, I did not know how to not end it.

"Okay then, I have to go, my rickshaw is waiting."

"Okay. Bye then," I said. I did not look into her eyes. While I could always see what was going on inside her through her eyes, for once I did not want her to see what was going on inside me through my eyes.

I quickly turned around and did not see her go. Correction, could not see her go. After walking a few steps, I turned around to check if she had not got stuck due to any reason. The concern for her was still alive in me, a part of me was dead in me. But she had left. The rickshaw and the hopes disappeared into the morning mist.

I walked back to the hostel with a blank mind. A bit worried like a parent whose child has gone away. A bit relieved like an athlete who has just finished a race. A bit broken like a student who had failed an exam but glad that the struggle was over.

As I entered my room, still not knowing how to react, a text message displayed:

"You know you are one of the most special persons in my life. But… but, I will never be able to show this to you. I don't know what to say more. Please, like always, this time also understand without me saying."

Add another feeling. Felt a bit happy like a general who had lost the battle but was confident about winning the war.

"I understand genius. Take care."

Wish words could do justice to what I felt then. But glad that again there were no words that could do justice.

* * *

As I read through the last line, Rohit came over. His face was red with anger as if he wanted to say a lot of things but didn't know where to start. This was the first time that I had seen him angry. I got the message but wanted to calm him down.

"Nice writing, buddy. Let me also show you what I have written in my notes inspired by your habit of writing a diary."

Rohit continued to stare at me, his eyes red as if the volcano were still burning inside him.

After 10 seconds, he said,

"Next time, don't!" with a lot of effort. And he left the room.

I realized my fault and was glad with Rohit's sense to control his temper and not create a scene.

We never discussed this incident again.

However, his diary did hint towards the reason behind his seemingly quite behavior.

7

Interlude - 2

Prashant: "Interesting writing by Rohit and impressive management by you. Though slightly strict one, I would say."

Saahas: "Rather seemingly very strict. Trouble was brewing, the support was fluid. An explosion could have taken time. And it did."

Prashant: "Didn't you see it coming?"

Saahas: "You always see it coming, but at times don't realize it."

Prashant: "Intense words."

Saahas: "And so were the events."

8

Abhimanyu - 1

One Monday morning, Subbu came to the training hall before the sessions for the day were scheduled to begin:

"Good morning, everyone! My name is Subbu in case you have forgotten because of the Monday blues."

We all laughed.

"I thought why not come over and speak to you about something that makes you forget your Monday blues."

We all got excited. He continued,

"So, all of you have made good progress in the training. I hope we all agree."

"Yes," a few voices spoke out.

"Great. Now to check how good the progress has been, we are going to begin with your evaluation from next week. Going forward, every alternate Monday, you will not have any classes in the morning. Instead, we will have an evaluation for three subjects each Monday, with the evaluation for each subject lasting 1 hour."

There was stunned silence. It was a surprise for all of us.

"The format will include both subjective and objective questions. The evaluation records will be shared with your HR."

The silence got graver.

"Let me know if you have any questions." After a long silence, Binoy, who was sitting next to me, said,

"Subbu, I think Monday blues were better."

Everyone laughed. Subbu then left the hall for the sessions of the day to begin.

After the morning sessions, while all of us were still in the training hall, Kamal came to me and asked,

"Can you not ask Subbu to postpone the tests?"

"And why should I ask Subbu to do so?" I reverted.

"Because you are our representative," he quickly responded.

"Okay. But that is not going to be a convincing reason for Subbu to postpone, other than that of me being the representative. Can we have a better reason?"

"Because we need more time to prepare," Binoy remarked.

"But shouldn't we all have been prepared from Day 1, considering training is the only thing we were expected to do here? Plus, we have a week."

"Correct," Pallavi said.

"But as our representative, isn't it your job to share our request with Subbu?" Kamal said, slightly agitated.

I was feeling good and bad at the same time. Good because Kamal was acknowledging the role of a representative, bad because he was imposing his demands.

"Correct," I reverted.

"Then why don't you ask Subbu?" Binoy added.

"I have to share the batch's requirements with Subbu, not random requests. Let me know if everyone is against the evaluation. In case there is even a single person who wants the evaluation, we will proceed with the evaluation. Else, I will go and speak to Subbu. Is that fair?"

Binoy nodded, and Kamal gave a half nod. I continued.

"Those who are not in favor of the evaluation, please raise your hands."

Five people raised their hands. Rohit and Pallavi did not raise their hands.

"Great. People here want the evaluation to happen. So, let us prepare for that."

"But how do we prepare?" Kamal asked, more agitated now.

"Let us see, buddy." This time I was the one smiling.

The sessions continued after lunch. In the evening, Pallavi, Rohit and I went for our post-dinner evening walk.

"Smart move buddy. You played that well," Pallavi said during the evening walk.

"It was a good strategy. He knows that when you ask for responses and want the responses in your favor, always ask those who are against your proposal to raise their hands. People are typically reluctant to show up, thus the probability of the result being in your favor increases."

I smiled.

"You seemed to be fine when the evaluations were announced. Why so?" Pallavi asked.

"Because I had to. If I had shown that I am uncomfortable with this decision, more people would have objected to it. Personally, while I also feel this is going to be tough, I need to understand what is in the larger interest of the group and get others to act along those lines."

"Agreed," Pallavi responded.

"Is it a way for Subbu to impose discipline in the batch?" Rohit asked.

I simply shrugged my shoulders, which conveyed maybe or maybe not.

"Anyhow, while this evaluation is important, how are we going to prepare for it?" Pallavi asked.

I gave a bigger smile to Pallavi.

"You will get to know tomorrow."

And the three of us walked back.

* * *

Next morning, it was time to open my diary. Before the morning sessions could begin, I went in front of the class. I spoke.

"How many of us think we are prepared for the tests?" I asked.

"Not another one of your polls, Saahas," Kamal reverted.

"One more time, buddy. I promise, the second-last one for the week."

"So, how many of us think we are prepared for the evaluation? Please raise your hands."

Nineteen people did not raise their hands. The only one who did raise his hand was Rohit.

Everyone laughed at seeing me not raise my hand because the general sense was that I was prepared for the evaluation and that is why I did not object the day before.

"So, while we cannot avoid the evaluation, we can be better prepared for it. I am proposing that apart from the regular self-preparation we will do, we should also do peer-to-peer learning sessions." Ten seconds of silence.

"Sounds interesting. But how does that help?" Binoy reverted.

"Good question. So, we have folks from Mechanical, Electrical, and Electronics backgrounds. I suggest that folks from Mechanical pick up their topics and teach folks from Electrical and Electronics, and similarly for folks from Electrical and for folks from Electronics. Starting tomorrow, i.e. Wednesday, till Friday, we can have a one-hour session each in the evening. And over the weekend, everyone can do group study or self-study as convenient. Through this, not only will everyone learn, but the one who is taking the peer-to-peer session will also have a greater understanding of his or her concepts."

"That's a great idea," Kamal reverted. I was surprised for once by his agreement on something that I was proposing.

"Now to the last poll of the week. Who is going to volunteer to take up the peer-to-peer sessions?"

Luckily, five people raised their hands. On requesting the need for three volunteers only, two people put their hands down. Rohit and two more folks were the volunteers.

"Great. Thank you for volunteering. I will seek the permissions to allow us an extra hour in this room every evening. And one more thing," I continued.

"To date, I have been noting down the key learnings from whatever we have been taught every day. I will share that with everyone for ready reference as required."

"Thank you for that," Kamal said.

And so, from the next day, we began. The approach, despite some initial hiccups, mostly related to volunteers not being able to answer the questions completely, worked, and the mood was relatively calm in the hostel on Sunday evening.

Except that Kamal and Binoy were keeping some distance from me. Maybe they felt that I could have avoided the upcoming Monday misery.

The tests on Monday went well, and most of the batch seemed happy with their performance.

On Thursday afternoon, I went to check with Subbu to see if he had had a chance to evaluate how the group had performed as a whole, considering that the individual evaluations were going to be kept confidential.

He just smiled back and said,

"Much better than someone on a paid holiday would have performed."

9

Abhimanyu - 2

One evening, after the sessions for the day had ended and we were about to leave the hall, Subbu came in front of the class. He had his all-too-familiar smile, which meant trouble.

"Guys, I hope you enjoyed preparing for the evaluation."

There wasn't any response.

He continued to smile and added,

"I know, I know, no one likes to be evaluated. Even after all these years, even I don't like it."

We all laughed.

"But it is important, so instead of thinking about whether do or not to do, let us continue with it."

Again, stunned silence.

"However," he continued. "There is another engagement that I have lined up for all of you. This will be in a group. All of you will be put into groups of 4, so five groups of four people each and will have to deliver a project on the topic in 2 weeks. The groups have been decided by me."

People were divided into groups to ensure there was a mix of people from different branches of engineering in each group. Binoy and Pallavi were in one group, Kamal and I were in one, and Rohit was with others.

"How will the topics be decided, Subbu?" I asked.

"You decide. By selecting from one of the topics that I will share." Not sure if that seemed like our decision or his decision.

So Subbu put out seven topics on a slide and asked everyone to give their first and second preference. There wasn't any clash in the selection of topics, and each group got a topic of their preference.

The topic chosen by Binoy and Pallavi's group was related to 'Electrical design aspects of power plants', which was more inclined to Binoy's area of interest.

The presentations were to be delivered in front of the Managing Director of the Thermal Plant in Nagpur, who was going to visit the campus in 2 weeks.

Everyone started working on the presentation in focused groups in the evening. A couple of days later, during the evening walk, I asked Pallavi and Rohit how things were shaping up.

Rohit seemed fine. He said, "You and I have updated so many presentations over the last few weeks, this seems to be just another one."

I asked Pallavi.

"Presentations are not the challenge, it's the people who you work with."

This was the first time I had heard Pallavi complain about anything or anyone. She generally was a happy-go-lucky kind of girl.

"Can't disagree. But what happened?" I asked.

"Nothing much. Let whatever happens in the group stay in the group." I decided not to pursue this further.

However, the next day I got involved, unwillingly.

Post-breakfast, Binoy came up to me and spoke agitatedly,

"Can we change the groups now?"

"Don't think it will be a good idea considering everyone has started making progress with their work. But why do you want to change the group?" I replied.

"Why do people change groups, Saahas?" Binoy asked, which seemed more like a comment rather than a question.

"For multiple reasons. Let me guess, is it the other people in your group?"

"Precisely."

"Or are you the person in the group?"

He gave me an angry look. Others around gave a small laugh, which agitated him more.

"Well, I don't think it is a good idea and suggest you resolve this among yourselves."

Binoy continued in his agitated mood. "But aren't you the leader? And the job of the leader is…"

"To create more leaders."

Before Binoy could complete or I could respond, Pallavi replied.

"Don't worry, Saahas, we will sort this out among ourselves."

In the evening, I went to Pallavi to check again what the issue was and how we could resolve it.

"The issue is among us. And I suggest you mind your own business," Pallavi said.

"Well, I would be happy not to intervene. But I would be happier if the issue is sorted."

"And I would be happiest if you stay out of it."

I was slightly taken aback by Pallavi's reaction. We had been on friendly terms, and I was coming in to resolve the issue. Maybe I was crossing a line which she had drawn. A line that Binoy wanted me to cross. However, I thought it better to stay away.

I never got to know what the issue was, nor did I try to get in. I did a status check with each of the group from time to time and updated Subbu.

Despite the initial hassles, the presentations and the subsequent questions and answers went well, and Subbu seemed quite happy with the efforts that everyone had put in. Rohit's group was recognized as the best one, followed by the team in which Kamal and I were. Mementos were given to Rohit's and our group. The Managing Director of the Thermal Plant also appreciated the efforts and said that he would take away some of the slides for colleagues in the thermal plant so that they could be used for their training.

In the evening, Binoy again came up to me.

"You know what, we could have been the winners today only if you had done your job."

"I am doing my job. And as far as I know, I am doing it decently well."

"Why don't you ask this question to the rest of the batch?"

Before I could respond, Rohit came in and said.

"While I don't know if Binoy got the answer, I think there is enough questioning done for the day with you. Let us call it a time out and discuss this sometime later."

However, this question was soon going to be asked, not to me, but to everyone.

* * *

Considering the last few weekends, everyone was busy preparing for the evaluations, so we all decided to go out for a party. It was the first one for the entire group and it was surprising that it took so long to happen.

It was Binoy's birthday as well, so he decided to take the lead in organizing the venue. We all agreed to contribute so as not to burden anyone financially.

We went on Saturday evening to the venue which had an exclusive hall for all of us. There was light music being played on the hall's music system. After the initial snacks, Binoy suggested playing a game. I looked at Pallavi and Rohit as if they knew what this was about. They just shrugged their shoulders, indicating that they did not have an idea. Binoy continued,

"Considering that we have all spent some time with each other and have gotten to know each other, it would be good if we share what we think about others."

This sounded interesting.

"But won't people be diplomatic?" Rohit asked before Binoy could finish.

Binoy continued,

"That is why the responses will be anonymous. There will be a box placed on the table. Pages and pens are kept on another table. You can write whatever you want to write about any other person, mentioning the name of the person at the top. Hope that is clear."

"Binoy, that is fine. However, I suggest everyone not to use any offensive language," I said candidly.

"Yes, Mr. Representative. And in case someone does, I will filter myself. Now let us begin."

Everyone started writing and putting the papers in the box. After 15 minutes, Binoy asked,

"Is anyone left?"

There wasn't any response. So Binoy decided to go ahead with the opening of the boxes.

He started reading aloud. Rohit also joined Binoy on stage. Looking at this, Binoy remarked,

"Don't worry. I will read only what is written," to which everyone laughed.

The first one was of Pallavi. So Binoy decided to read out all the papers for Pallavi.

"P.T. Usha of our batch," read one.

"The dynamic one," read another. "A pleasure playing with you on the field. Thank you for inspiring," read another one. "Cute girl with big muscles," read yet another one. "Thank you everyone!" shouted out Pallavi. "Bossy lady," read the final one.

"Thank you too early?" I remarked to Pallavi. "Never mind," she smiled. "By the way, wait for yours," she said with a bigger smile.

Next up was Kamal.

"Our Rambo" attributing to his visit to the gym. "The outlier of the batch" read another one. "The rule breaker" read another one. "Stay different!" read another one. Kamal gave a pleasing smile and nodded.

Binoy was next, so Rohit read that out,

"Wish you could be our representative," came the first one," Binoy smiled, looking at me. I smiled back, saying,

"This seems to be more of a comment for me rather than a compliment for you." Everyone laughed.

"Appreciate your friendly nature," said one. "Good to know someone so chill," said the other.

And it continued for others. Finally, it was me,

"The wolf who lives for the pack", "The leader without a title", "The 2 am friend".

Those were pleasant surprises. "Why are you giving me book titles?" I candidly remarked.

"What do you think of yourself?" That was not pleasant but surprising.

"Stop dictating terms." That was neither pleasant nor surprising.

Rohit and I were sitting together. Rohit tapped on my shoulder, looking at the feedback. I just smiled back.

Post the game, we all danced to some music, had dinner, and went back to the hostel. We walked from our cabs to the hostel gate. Rohit, Pallavi, and I were together, like most of the time. Rohit sensed I was not feeling great with the feedback just received. Before he could say anything, Pallavi said, "You don't seem too happy with the feedback, Saahas."

I rephrased, "Would you have been happy with that kind of feedback?"

"Yes. Because I would look at the positive things that people said and ignore the negative ones. I think that is one of the major reasons for our miseries. Looking at what we don't have rather than what we have," she remarked in her usual style.

I just nodded.

Rohit added, "Don't worry, you are doing the right thing."

"I know I am. But don't think others feel the same thing," I reverted.

Rohit added, "A reformist does not have to be a populist, my friend."

I reverted, "A reformist cannot be a populist, my friend." We all laughed and went back to the hostel.

10

Interlude - 3

Prashant: "That seemed to be an interesting game. I think we should have such games in the corporate world as well."

Saahas: "Not sure if you could afford the outcome."

Prashant (Laughs): "I am sure not."

He sipped water from the glass placed in front of him and continued.

Prashant: "So, overall everything seemed to be going fine. Such incidents are one-off, but I don't think this was anything major."

Prashant paused and then continued.

Prashant: "I think we are digressing. So, Mr. Yudhishthira of Mahabharata, or should I call you Arjun."

Saahas: "Abhimanyu."

Prashant laughed.

Prashant: "Whichever character you want. Then what happened?"

Saahas: "Then when everything is going well, what does the management do?"

Prashant: "What do we do?"

Saahas: "It changes."

Prashant: "Sorry?"

Saahas: "Although for some other reason, finally, someone is."

Prashant: "I did not get you. What had happened?"

Saahas: "When everything was going fine, the 'representative' was asked to step down."

Prashant: "By?"

Saahas (Wondering if he is serious or if he is making fun of me): "By you, the management."

11
Shakuni - 1

Mr. Akhilendra Sharma or Akhil, as he was called, was the General Manager with the Company at the Chhattisgarh plant. He was supposed to come to visit CPTI as part of the 'Leadership Connect' initiative, during which senior managers from the power plants of the company were to come and meet the trainees. The purpose was twofold,

a. Share the updates on the company

b. Know about the journey of the trainees and how well they were progressing

The latter part was important considering the amount of resources being invested by the company for training the new engineers.

We had met Akhil during one of the initial orientation sessions at the Chhattisgarh plant. He came across as someone who was easily approachable and also someone who knew his stuff and what he wants. Around 5 feet 5 inches in height and someone who seemingly does not get too much time to focus on his physical health.

Akhil, in fact, came early to our hostel instead of going to the training hall, half an hour before the scheduled session. We were surprised to see him. He said he had come over to catch up over breakfast as he was bored of eating the same hotel food again and again.

We would have killed each other for one meal at the hotel he was staying. I looked at Rohit and said, "Maybe this is how successful we want to be. Getting bored of meals from 5-star hotels."

Kamal was seated next to Akhil, and both of them started chatting. Akhil nodded and gave a smile at whatever Kamal said, which made Kamal even more expressive. Both of them seemed to be having a good conversation. Akhil also interacted with a few of us and ended by saying that considering we did not want to have breakfast until lunch, he would catch up with the rest of us during the day's session.

For once, I did not have to pull everyone to the session because Akhil was there. We started the session on time, and Akhil began:

"Good morning, everyone. My name is Akhil and good to see all twenty of you again."

We all laughed. He continued.

"I am here to take you through the developments at our plant and share some knowledge about the industry. I am sure you have received a lot of it in the past few months. But before I begin, I would like to tell you that this is the most enjoyable phase of your career."

He continued,

"I remember my days as a trainee early in my career 15 years ago. Rather, I remember those times fondly. And I also know that you are surprised that I have worked for 15 years. I know, I look like someone who has worked for 30 years. I know I might not talk like one."

We all laughed again. This time Akhil himself was leading the laughter at his self-deprecating joke. It was amazing to see that a person with so much experience was so secure that he was able to crack jokes on himself. We had another metric for success.

"So, this is how we have planned the day. I will take you through some of the industry developments and the company developments for around 2 hours. We will then take a 15-minute drinks break. Then we will play a game for 30 minutes. After that, we will take a lunch break. We will assemble post lunch to know the results of the game. After the game, I will go and meet Subbu and the rest of the management of the institute and catch my train in the evening."

We were all excited, not as much for the session as for the game.

Akhil then began his session on the power sector and company developments. What was interesting about his session on sector developments was that what he was sharing was more contemporary and global, such as developments in the renewable energy sector, electric vehicles, and green hydrogen. He also discussed non-technical stuff like how policy and regulatory developments impact and enable the growth of the sector. He shared the history of developments in the sector and what needs to be done to take the sector forward.

While the training in the institute was of good quality with the professors, it was more technical in nature and largely related to what is happening within a power plant. What Akhil was showing us was the world outside the plant. We might not be working on some of the areas for maybe the next few years, but these areas were going to impact our work nonetheless. And his style of delivering the presentation was making it all the more fun.

The session was engaging with hardly any dull moments in between. Akhil ended his presentation and asked,

"So how did you like the presentation?"

Kamal replied, "It felt like a story."

For once, everyone agreed with him.

Akhil smiled and said, "That is how presentations should be. They are a tool to deliver your message, not the message itself, which should require a wake-up alarm."

We all laughed.

As shared earlier, Akhil asked us to take a 15-minute break. We all left the room for water and a bit of a stroll. Akhil continued working on his laptop in the hall.

We came back after 10 minutes. Akhil was impressed by the discipline and said,

"Don't worry. I will let you enjoy the remaining 5-minute break as well, and then we start."

After 5 minutes, he started

"And the next session is about…"

A long silence because this was not the plan. The plan was a game.

"Don't worry folks. I am kidding. As I said, we will play a small game. And the name of the game is 'Team Check'. And for this, I would like all of you to take out your phones. Please expect the unexpected." He smiled. A sarcastic one now. This seemed interesting.

He continued.

"I will be putting up some questions on the screen. There will be a six-digit code along with the question. It is the same code for all the questions. You have to go to the website mentimeter.com. Fill in the code and start answering. Let me assure you of two things:

The answers will be anonymous. Even I could not see who gave what reply.

There are no right or wrong answers, as you would realize upon seeing the questions.

"So are we good to go?" he asked everyone.

"Yes, Akhil," Binoy replied.

"Good. Let's start."

The first question came up with the options:

1. "What is the best thing about the training?"

    a.   The knowledge being gained

    b.   The campus

    c.   The city's food

    d.   Free money

We all laughed. This was going to be fun. Each one of us opened the website mentimeter.com, filled in the six-digit code, and marked our option. Since Akhil had asked to fill the best option, we could enter only one.

Akhil asked after 30 seconds.

"Is everyone done? I ask because I can see on my laptop only eighteen have filled in. Okay, now we are twenty. Good, let us now proceed to the next one."

We were expecting the answers as well; otherwise, where is the fun?

"Akhil. Where can we see the responses?" Pallavi asked.

"Good question. I can see the responses. Though I cannot see who has filled which option for anonymity reasons. I will share the responses and discuss these with you after lunch. Is that fair?"

"Sure," Pallavi replied.

Akhil continued with the next question:

  2.   "What do you miss most about college?"

    a.   Buddies

    b.   Afternoon naps

   c. Professors and learning

   d. Mess food

Again, laughter echoed through the hall.

He moved to the next question after half a minute when everyone had filled in their responses.

3. "How do you chill? (multiple options)"

   a. Watching movies

   b. Reading

   c. Physical activity

   d. Talking to family

   e. I am myself chill

We were quite surprised by the candor of the questions. But the real fun was about to begin.

He asked five more questions on a similar theme. He then moved on to slightly business stuff.

9. "How well do you feel this training has enriched your power sector skills?"

   a. A lot

   b. Somewhat

   c. Not at all

   d. Didn't know that is what we came here for

Slight laughter in the hall, lower in volume than the previous one. He paused for 30 seconds. When everyone had filled in their options, he moved on.

10. "How has your experience been at the institute?

    a. Learning one

    b. Fun one

    c. Mixed bag

30 seconds' wait, and he moved to the next one.

11. "On a scale of 1-10, how would you rate your technical skills in the power sector today?"

    a. 8-10

    b. 4-7

    c. 0-3

    d. Minus

Akhil waited for 30 seconds and moved to the next one. He asked three questions on a similar theme.

And then the theme of the questions changed. The ultimate stuff was kept for last.

15. "How would you rate your experience with your representative?"

    a. Disciplined

    b. Casual

    c. Freedom

    d. Unfair

Akhil added that to ensure fair responses, I could not vote for this one and the next two questions. For once, I felt I had done something wrong and was worried about being singled out. But I thought it was fair considering the type of question to avoid conflict. Considering there were 30 seconds to respond, everyone except one voted.

He moved to the next one after 30 seconds:

16. "How effective has the representative been in ensuring things are on track?"

    a. Highly Effective

    b. Not at all effective

    c. Indifferent

I started feeling a bit embarrassed. But this was not new for me. Rohit put his hands on my shoulder and said, "Don't worry." I murmured that I am not because I simply cannot do anything. Akhil didn't notice this and moved to the next one after 30 seconds. The best or rather the worst one for the last:

17. "Do you want to change the representative?"

    a. Yes

    b. No

There was a huge silence. Pallavi had a surprised expression on her face. I was also surprised but thought better of it not to express anything.

"30 seconds, folks. And I am out of the way of your lunch," Akhil smiled. For some reason, his smile seemed less pleasant now.

Like the last two questions, everyone except one responded.

Akhil thanked everyone and said, "I hope we all had fun."

"No one had more fun than me, Akhil. Thank you," I said slowly. Only Rohit could hear it. He gave me a calming and assuring look. "Don't worry," he said.

Akhil added that he was going to have lunch with a friend in the city and would meet us after an hour.

For some reason, when we were heading out of the hall for lunch, Kamal looked at me and smiled. This was the first time he had smiled at me in some days. I didn't deem it too important to respond. I just nodded.

At lunch, the usual hustle was missing. In between, Rohit said, "Apparently, Akhil was asking similar questions in different ways so that we do not bluff. He has adopted the technique that most of the MBA institutes adopt. He is smart."

We all looked at him and realized that he was actually correct.

We were looking forward to knowing the answers, and I was not sure if I wanted to know the answers to some of the questions. Not that I was seeking validation or had sought validation in any form from anyone, but maybe I had actually taken the tag of representative too seriously and had made it a part of my identity.

Maybe, as the representative, I was not expected to take tough decisions to focus on the output.

Maybe as a leader, I should still have taken those tough decisions to focus on the output.

12
Shakuni - 2

Post lunch, we all walked back to the hall. Typically, the sessions after lunch are the ones in which you struggle to stay awake. This time around, it was going to be the opposite.

Akhil came in on time. He asked everyone how they found the exercise pre-lunch.

Kamal responded, "Depends on the responses."

Everyone, including Akhil, laughed.

Akhil said, "Okay. Then let me not hold back the suspense and move to the responses. But before I share the responses, let me thank all of you for participating and remind you that all the responses are anonymous, even for me."

"As if we had an option not to respond," Pallavi said, and everyone laughed.

Akhil started showing the responses in the form of pie charts and graphs on the mentimeter in values and percentages as per settings that he had done on the mentimeter. He started with the first question and the responses.

1. "What is the best thing about the training?"

    a. The knowledge being gained - 5 responses

    b. The campus - 5 responses

    c. The city food - 6 responses

    d. Free money - 4 responses

Everyone laughed. Akhil said, "Good to see we have at least four honest people here." Everyone laughed harder. Akhil then asked, "Anyone has anything to say on the responses, especially those who said free money? I am sure those who have answered this will not."

Binoy raised his hand. Akhil nodded. Binoy started, "The knowledge being provided is among the best that we could get, with the professors being experts in their field. While back in engineering college, we did get good knowledge and training, this one is more focused."

Akhil nodded. He smiled and asked, "But don't you like the free money?"

Everyone laughed.

Binoy: "I do. Everyone would. But a. The question was the best thing and b. There could be other avenues to earn free money, but not for the knowledge."

"Smart answer," Akhil complimented Binoy. Binoy smiled and sat down.

Akhil continued with responses to the rest of the questions. Considering the options, there was laughter here and laughter there for each of the questions. It seemed everyone had forgotten the last few questions. Akhil hadn't. I couldn't.

After responses to other questions, Akhil came to question number 15.

15. " How would you rate your experience with the Class Representative?"

   a. Discipline - 10

   b. Casual - 2

   c. Freedom - 5

   d. Unfair - 2

Akhil added: "Well, if I had an option, even I would vote for discipline. It has been good to see how well you all have been responding since morning. Plus, we keep getting feedback from Mr. Suburaj and the authorities regarding the batch. While everyone might not like being disciplined, it is still important and impressive."

I could only smile. My first one in the last few hours.

He continued, "And on that note, we come to the last two questions."

16. "How effective has the representative been in ensuring things are on track?"

   a. Highly Effective - 14

   b. Not at all effective - 1

   c. Indifferent - 4

Akhil said, "Great to see this. Getting a majority approval from your peers is difficult. I can say it from my personal experience at least." Everyone laughed.

I felt glad and kind of happy that my experiments and determination to do the right thing were working. Or so it seemed.

Akhil moved to the last one.

17.   "Do you want to change the representative?"

    a.   Yes - 14

    b.   No - 5

Before I could absorb the dichotomy between the responses to questions 16 and 17, Akhil gave an even bigger shock.

"This is interesting. While the majority think that the representative is effective, the majority also wants to change it."

I was shocked. This was one of those moments where you knew what was coming but were not prepared for it. Even before I could absorb the responses, Akhil continued.

"So why not listen to the majority? Let us change the representative."

Silence across the hall. Even before I or someone else could absorb what had happened, Akhil continued. After digging in, he was twisting the knife.

"So, whom do you want to select? Saahas, why don't you propose your successor as we might call him or her."

It was difficult for me to comprehend what was going on. It took me some time before Rohit elbowed me to speak. Before I could, a couple of voices in the crowd had already prompted "Binoy."

"Kamal!" came another one. "Pallavi!" said another one. But clearly, there were more voices for Binoy.

I could not look around to see who these were. They were definitely not from Binoy. Plus, with multiple voices, it was difficult to know. All it did was take me back to the early days of the training when a different name was being echoed.

"Okay. So, I hear Binoy's name. Saahas, any name you would like to put forward?"

"Binoy should be good," I spoke with as much confidence as I could gather,.

"Okay. Then Binoy it is," Akhil confirmed.

"Should we check with Binoy as well?" Pallavi interjected.

Akhil looked slightly unpleased at this interjection since he had already confirmed the name.

"Sure. Binoy, do you have any objection?"

Binoy, who was sitting quietly, had a suppressed smile. "No, Akhil. It would be a pleasure to be the representative or rather the leader."

Akhil congratulated Binoy and said,

"Good luck to Binoy for his new role. And also, a big thank you to Saahas for what he has done in the last few months. A round of applause for both of them and for all of you."

Akhil's words were a bit soothing. But these were more like an ointment on a deep cut.

Akhil then thanked everyone for the day and said that he would have to leave for a discussion with the institute authorities. I remember him saying earlier in the day that he would have a train later in the evening. I was hoping against hope that he would come back and change his decision. But he did not. And it took me a few days to realize that ultimately the batch had taken the decision, not him. He was just an enabler.

In the evening, Rohit, Pallavi and I went for our usual evening walk. There was an unusual silence. Pallavi tried to break the silence by humming a tune. But there wasn't any response. Pallavi thought it's wiser to let the silence do the talking.

Rohit: "I am surprised by the results of the survey. I was not expecting fourteen people to vote against you."

Saahas: "Even I am surprised. I was not expecting even five people to vote for me."

All three of us smiled. A smile that tries to hide the disappointment but ends up revealing more of it.

We didn't say a word and quietly walked back to our rooms.

13

Interlude - 4

Prashant: "I always knew what happened. Akhil had briefed me on this. But I was not sure that this is how it had ended."

"Yes indeed. It was a moment of great pride for me," (sarcasm is evident in Saahas's voice). "Didn't Akhil brief you properly?"

"I am sure he did to the best of his ability, but maybe some of the details were lost in transfer."

"Yes. A lot of some of the details were lost in transfer."

Prashant has started feeling a bit agitated by the repeated sarcasm from Saahas.

"So why don't you fill in the details?"

Saahas looks at the clock and realizes there are only 5 minutes left in the scheduled time.

"Are we sure we have so much time? I heard you are quite particular about the time of your meetings."

"I would like to make an exception for once. Now, would you like to make an exception as well and proceed with what happened?"

"Nothing happened."

"Nothing?"

"Yes. Nothing."

14
Karan - 1

Binoy took over as the representative the following Monday.

Over the weekend, after Akhil had left, we continued with our regular activities of the gym, local market visit, and of course, cricket. The dynamics within the team did not seem to change post Akhil's departure. Some people did seem relieved, including Kamal. I, all along, kept pondering what went wrong. Or was I overthinking? I kept thinking about it, and while I could have discussed this with Rohit, I did not want to come across as someone who was not following the rules that someone else has set. I kept quiet, only externally; internally, the chatter was non-stop.

Before the first session on Monday morning, I went in front of everyone one more time and, as always, briefed them on what lay ahead. I told them about the scheduled program for the week and said that, as shared by Akhil, Binoy was going to lead the batch going forward. There was a round of applause, which I am still not sure was because of what I had done or because Binoy was going to be the one leading. Binoy stood up from where he was sitting and said

"Thank you for the opportunity, folks. Just to correct Saahas, I am going to be the representative of the batch going forward."

I sat in my seat and for once felt a burden off my shoulders. But I'm not sure this is how I would have wanted it to end.

The sessions for the day proceeded without any major incidents.

In the evening, as Rohit, Pallavi and I went on our regular evening walk, I was quite quiet, which was unlike me. That's when I could not resist and asked both of them.

"So how is the mood in the camp, folks?" I asked to break the silence.

Pallavi, being quick-witted, said,

"You tell. How would you have felt if you got rid of a supervisor like you."

Both Rohit and I laughed. Pallavi continued.

"You yourself have given the answer. The camp is relieved."

I was not sure how to react. We continued our walk, enjoying the cool autumn breeze. Just before we went back to our rooms, Pallavi added:

"By the way, apart from feeling relieved, there is another feeling that is slightly uneasy. The group feels that they would not be as disciplined and focused as they had been with you. With you, everyone felt they could never fail."

For once, I also felt relieved.

* * *

The sessions continued as usual for the next few days.

On Friday, Subbu invited the director of a power plant in Madhya Pradesh, Mr. Vikas Nagpal, for a guest session. Mr. Nagpal was a batchmate of Subbu during his graduation days and had grown up in Nagpur. In his personal capacity, Subbu invited him to come over and have a session with us. Subbu had informed Binoy in advance regarding the guest session and asked him to communicate to the entire batch to be on time.

We all reached the hall before time and got seated. However, with a slight difference, there was no one in the first row. People looked at me, and I gave back a puzzled look.

Kamal spoke up, "Since he is no longer the representative, he will not sit in the first row."

I thought of responding but then dropped the idea to avoid escalation. Though it is better for him to stay in a sense of mystery. Pallavi didn't want the mystery to remain, so she said:

"Saahas is no longer obligated to. He can sit wherever he likes."

Before Kamal could respond, Subbu entered the hall along with Mr Nagpal. He wished everyone and introduced Mr Nagpal. He mentioned their friendship and how they have stayed in touch for more than 15 years despite not being in the same city. He invited Mr Nagpal to say a few words about his experience, which would be followed by a question and answer session.

Before Mr Nagpal could begin, Subbu noticed the empty first benches. He glanced at Binoy with an angry look. Binoy responded with a wry smile. Next, he glanced at me. I responded with the same puzzled look. Pallavi got the cue and decided to move to the front desk. Another person moved up along with her. But the damage was done.

Mr. Nagpal introduced himself and talked about his career journey, his current work profile, the challenges he has faced in his 15+ year career, and how he unwinds. He also shared some of the mistakes he had made in his career, which have made him a better person. Overall, he spoke for 20 minutes, but his frank and down-to-earth nature didn't allow for many dull moments.

He then asked everyone for questions. There was a pin-drop silence. Let alone anyone not asking any questions. No one even seemed to try. Subbu nudged everyone to feel free and frank to ask questions as Mr. Nagpal, while he was a director at a large power plant, he was here in his personal capacity.

Still a pin-drop silence.

This was turning out to be embarrassing for Subbu and the batch. Subbu tried to do some face-saving and stepped in with a question.

"Mr. Vikas…"

"It's fine Subbu, you don't need to be formal. You can call me Vikas," Mr. Nagpal interjected. We all smiled. We also realized that while none of us was speaking, the only person, that too not from the batch who decided to speak was stopped in between.

Subbu continued, "Vikas. We did our undergraduate together and today you have become a big director in a big firm. While I am a small lecturer in a big institute. What has been your secret to success?"

Mr Nagpal smiled and responded.

"Well, the secret has been that there is no secret. In fact, even before I answer that, let me tell you that a big post or a big salary might not always define success. Your parameters for success might be different from mine. If you are getting time to spend with your family, in a lush green campus and an opportunity to create future leaders, that might be a bigger success than being amongst the senior management in a large company. That does not mean you do not strive for bigger things in life, but you must strive for better things with balance."

"Now having defined what success means, let me answer your question considering that you are asking me how I reached the level of senior management of a big company."

Mr. Nagpal continued, "Every day you need to realize that each one of us is fighting our own battles. Everyone has issues in their personal lives and professional lives. The person sitting next to you in the public transport is fighting his/her battles, the person sitting next to you in this session is fighting his/her battles."

Everyone started looking at the person sitting next to them, and there was laughter. He continued,

"You need to realize that those who can balance their battles will go up. For example, if you focus on your personal issues, you might be able to resolve them but at the cost of professional growth. If you focus on your professional journey, you would achieve growth in your career but your family life might get affected. There is a cost for everything and it all depends on what cost you are willing to bear. I chose to focus on my professional journey but pay the cost of not seeing my kids grow up, not being with my parents as they grew old, not spending much time with my spouse and this is how I achieved the so-called success."

As Mr. Nagpal finished, Subbu asked if anyone has any questions. Again, there was pin-drop silence for 10 seconds.

Finally, Kamal spoke up:

"How have you planned your career trajectory?" The question seemed similar to what Subbu had asked, but it was a question from one of us nonetheless.

Mr. Nagpal responded, "You don't plan your career, you plan each day and to the extent possible each hour. I never worked thinking I wanted to be something big. I always focused on the next task at hand and ensuring I did it well with complete dedication and sincerity. I stuck to the basics of being punctual with tasks assigned, being open and transparent in communication, and being ethical. Whatever work was assigned to me and in whichever department, I always felt I have given my 99% no matter what others said. And I would realize that I am yet to give 100% and that would give me the motivation to keep trying harder every other day at every task. We need to focus on things that we can control and let go of things, however difficult it may seem, that we cannot control."

Kamal thanked him and sat down.

Again, there was a pin-drop silence. Each instance of pin-drop silence seemed more deafening than the earlier one.

Subbu looked at his watch and saw that 55 minutes had passed for the session. While there was still some time to go, he decided to call it off based on the response. He thanked Mr. Nagpal for coming over and gave him a small memento. Everyone stood up and gave a round of applause to Mr. Nagpal. For some reason, he didn't seem too happy. However, he thanked everyone and was escorted out of the room with Subbu.

The rest of the sessions throughout the day went in a normal way, with a slight difference. The first bench was empty again.

* * *

In the evening, while we were returning to our accommodation from the hall, Subbu called out to Binoy.

After dinner, Binoy came up to me and asked if he could join me for the evening walk alone. I was a bit surprised by the request but didn't see any harm in it. I told Pallavi and Rohit about it, and Binoy and I went for a walk.

We started with casual interactions about the weather and the training. Binoy then came to the point.

"I have been made this representative or whatever you would like to call it. I was keen to take up this role and was excited when I was chosen, considering others had voted for me. But now I find it kind of overwhelming. There are a lot of interests to balance."

I was totally surprised. I thought these were still early days and he was enjoying the role. He continued.

"Subbu called me to his room in the evening when we were coming back."

"Yes. I saw that."

"He was fairly disappointed with the morning session."

"Why? The session was good."

"Are you trying to act funny? Because if you are, you are not being one," he candidly remarked.

"Okay. Carry on."

"Subbu wasn't happy with the session in terms of the way we responded. He said that we seemed disinterested and this shows poorly on the batch. There should have been someone to take the lead, get others to occupy the front benches and ask questions, even if they might sound not too good."

He continued.

"He even gave your example of how you asked Gopal Sir questions a few months back, which was quite evident were being framed on the spot. You were looking lost while asking the question, but it was appreciated that you at least tried."

I smiled and then it disappeared.

"Okay. I did what I thought was right. But I'm not sure how I can help. If, as a representative of the batch, you want me to take the initiative on various activities, I would follow your command. Not sure what else I could do."

"No. We all know that and know you will do whatever seems correct, but that is not where I want your help right now. I want your help on how to manage all this."

I thought about what to tell him considering that the situation seemed funny. The person because of whom I was seemingly in pain for the last 5 days was asking me to rescue him. Believing in Karma, I once again did what I thought was the right thing, to give him fair advice.

"Take Charge."

He gave it a deep thought and said, "Okay. Let me try."

15

Karan - 2

Binoy was on the task from the next week. As we all entered the hall and started getting seated, he skipped his seat with Kamal and sat at the front desk. Subbu came in and seemed surprised. The rest of us seemed even more surprised. Subbu, while being surprised, was also happy that Binoy had heeded his feedback.

The weather had started turning a bit cold in Nagpur or, as they say, the heat was reducing in Nagpur. It was time for the local cricket tournaments to begin. We were informed by Subbu during one of the evening sessions that he was approached by his friends about a local tennis cricket ball tournament in case we would like to proceed. He said he would also be a part of the team.

We all thought it was a great idea. We had to apply on a website. Binoy also decided to be a part of the cricket tournament, skipping the gym. He was apparently trying to take the initiative to another level, which seemed like a good thing. The first thing that the website asked for was a name and the captain. Rohit proposed the name 'Powerful'. It felt awful for a cricket team. Subbu proposed 'Power Engineers'. We didn't want to say no to Subbu upfront, so I asked others to provide another name. Pallavi said, "Victors." Everyone liked it. So, we put the name.

The difficult part being done, then came the more difficult part of selecting a captain. Binoy thought about raising his hand but decided others should also get a chance to explore leadership roles. We all looked at Subbu. Subbu said he would love to but wanted to have a young leader, rather a relatively young leader. Rohit took Pallavi's name. Suddenly there was unanimous agreement, except from Pallavi. We all looked at her. She stayed silent for 5 seconds and then said okay. However, she said,

"All this is fine. But don't expect me to be an idealistic leader. I am not someone who says 'If we win credit goes to the team and if we lose what was I doing there'. I say that we swim and sink together." And she looked at me.

Everyone laughed and looked at me.

Pallavi passed an apologetic smile at me. I smiled back saying, "It's fine. I am used to this now."

Everyone laughed again.

The tournament was on next weekend with sixteen teams, with each game being a 10-over each side knockout. Pallavi performed well with her medium-pace bowling and quick running. We reached the finals but lost. We were disappointed but still had our heads held high when Pallavi went to receive the runners-up trophy. After the cricket tournament, we decided to have a small party to celebrate the success. This time around there were no games.

* * *

Next Monday, as per his usual schedule, Subbu shared the agenda for the week. There were some simulator trainings lined up for the week. The purpose of the simulator was to give a real-life experience of operating a power plant to everyone.

We were split into two groups of ten members each considering the number of simulators. The first group would use the simulator in the first half, and the second group in the second half, post lunch. Meanwhile, the other group would engage in self-study, which was a pseudonym for 'Chilling'. For each group of 10, everyone would perform on the simulator in pairs.

As luck would have it, Pallavi and Binoy were again in the same group, though larger ones of ten people each this time around. While the first couple of days everything was fine, on the third day, Pallavi had a disagreement with one of the group members on the ramp-up rate of the power plant. The disagreement quickly ramped up into an argument.

Looking at things getting heated up, Binoy decided to intervene. However, Pallavi, being Pallavi, asked him clearly not to intervene. Binoy, wanting to resolve the issue, still decided to go ahead, not being mindful that both of them had shared an unpleasant incident in the very recent past.

Things heated up further, however not between Pallavi and her partner, but between Pallavi and Binoy.

"You know that is your problem," Pallavi said.

"I thought I was trying to be the solution here," Binoy reverted.

"And that is the problem."

Binoy and eight others were confused. Pallavi wasn't done, however.

"You don't seem to listen to the ladies. When I am saying that you should not intervene, you should not."

"But as a batch representative, I thought I should…"

"At least respect the other person's views." Pallavi did not let Binoy complete.

"Last time also, you were not willing to listen to others' viewpoints, especially when it comes from the ladies. While Saahas would do what he thinks is correct, he would at least respect and listen to others' opinions."

Binoy was slightly taken aback. He spoke,

"I don't think this is supposed to be a comparison between Saahas and me. And let us not bring up the past. Fine if both of you want to continue to argue, let me not be a party or an escalating agent. But more importantly, let me not be the dummy target."

Before Pallavi could say anything, the lab assistant who had gone to the washroom while this commotion was going on came in, and everyone went back to their simulators. Pallavi and her partner discussed their disagreement with the lab assistant, and he sorted it out. Everyone wished that the assistant could have rescheduled his break.

* * *

During the week, the simulator trainings went on as usual. Binoy was informed that Raghuvendra and Samar from Human Resources were going to come on campus for an interaction with everyone the following week. We thought it was still early considering the last visit by Akhil was just a month back, but this wasn't our call.

The next day, Raghu and Samar reached the hall at 10 am. It was actually good to see them after a long time.

Raghu greeted everyone and began sharing his agenda for the visit.

"We are here to just catch up with everyone. We keep receiving feedback about how your training is progressing from Subbu. We also hear that you do give Subbu tough times in between, but we understand that is part of the process. We wanted to know considering there are only a few weeks left for your training and in case anyone has any suggestions or feedback on the training, we would love to hear."

Everyone was surprised to hear the feedback from Subbu. A bigger surprise was, however, in store.

Samar spoke up,

"Excuse me,"

Raghu replied,

"Samar, this was for the trainees. I don't think you are also one of the trainees. At least not in the last few months."

Everyone laughed.

Samar replied with a smile. He did not take offense and took the comment lightly. However, Samar replied.

"Raghu, I like your sense of humor. But I had an observation. Out of twenty trainees, only nineteen are present here. Where did one go?"

The surprise was here. It was not long before everyone realized Kamal was the missing person.

Samar spoke up, "The missing person is Kamal. But he is yet to be found."

Before the mystery could deepen, Raghu asked Binoy, "So, Binoy. Where is Kamal?"

Binoy casually said,

"He has gone home for a personal visit. He had a relative from overseas coming over, and he has gone to see them. He will come back after two days."

Before anyone could react, Raghu said,

"And when were we going to be told about this? After he would come back?" He was soft but firm.

Binoy replied,

"No. He had informed me last week. Due to other activities over the weekend, I missed informing you," he remarked casually.

Raghu was boiling up because of the casual attitude. It was reflecting on his face but he did not let it reflect in his voice. Maybe that is what an experienced professional is all about.

"This is indiscipline in my opinion. I remember up until a few months back, any person, if going even for half a day off, let alone someone from the company visiting or not, would inform us. And here, even after he has left, we don't know."

Samar added, "Has this happened in the past as well?"

Binoy said, "No. This was the first time so that is why I missed it."

Raghu now raised his voice.

"But the first time should not have happened. No matter who you are at what level, how senior or junior, you need to learn to respect the time of others, no matter whether senior or junior to you. I feel we have wasted our time here. We came here for 'Nothing.'"

Binoy was quiet as he wanted Raghu to cool down. Instead, Rohit came in.

"No Raghu. We understand your concern. We assure you this is the only time this has happened. And we hope it should not happen again."

Raghu closed by saying, "It better not."

Raghu and Samar continued with their interaction with the batch. They asked about our key learnings and, since they were going to repeat this program for the next batch of GETs, what changes could be made. They requested everyone to be frank. Initially, as is often the case, no one responded. Then they went around asking one by one, and everyone opened up.

Raghu and Samar also shared stories about the activities in the plant and how things were moving well. They also shared how Amitabh was closely watching the progress of trainings and that is why repeatedly sending folks to visit the trainees.

In the evening, everyone went out for dinner with Raghu and Samar. Raghu and Samar told stories about their families, graduation days, and the learning and training methodologies that have developed in a relatively short span of 10 years. Some of us also shared about our families, what is special about the places where we came from, and our keen interests. Rohit and Samar connected well over their love for writing.

Next day, Samar and Raghu interacted with Gopal Sir along with Subbu and left in the afternoon. Binoy went to see them off from the institute's entrance.

Kamal came back the next day from his hometown, and Binoy told him about the interactions. Kamal asked him to relax and said that such things keep happening.

The training continued for four more weeks, with the last week focusing more on presentations and sharing our key learnings from the past 6 months. Subbu was quite impressed with some of the presentations and mentioned that he would include some of them in his teaching material.

16

Interlude - 5

Prashant: "You all seemed to be having a good time. So?"

Saahas: "So?"

"Go on"

"Nothing much. As I mentioned, the activities kept moving on their normal course, without any major surprises or events. At the end of the 6-month training, Binoy went to the Chhattisgarh plant and I went to the plant in Jodhpur. Kamal and Pallavi went to the same plant as Binoy while Rohit and I were together. There was no more requirement of a representative or a leader, as everyone was reporting to their individual reporting managers at the plants, whether you liked the manager or not."

"Do you think Binoy did a good job?" Prashant asked.

I was surprised by him seeking my opinion on this. "Frankly, I am not the right person to comment on it. But since you asked, all I would like to say is that he did his job and I did my job."

"I never asked about how you did your job. Still, you mean to say he acted as a representative and you acted as a leader."

"Again, I will be biased if I say anything like that. Ultimately, you deliver as you perceive your role to be."

A long pause. This one was a comfortable one.

"Have you and Binoy stayed in touch?"

"Not much. But not because we did not want to, but because we could not. We are a part of the common group and do exchange common greetings on birthdays/festivities, but nothing much beyond that."

"That is fair. Even I am part of an extended family WhatsApp group and share a similar relationship with the members."

Both of us laughed.

"And what about Pallavi and Rohit?"

"Yes. We talk on a regular basis and still have the evening walk but over a video call."

Prashant smiled. But he wasn't done yet. And neither was Saahas.

Saahas: "And didn't you miss something?"

"About?"

"Binoy and Kamal?"

"What?"

"Exactly. What happened after Raghu and Samar came back from Nagpur?"

"So, you know something happened. Well, 'Nothing' happened; he and Kamal were separately reprimanded for indiscipline."

"What kind of indiscipline? Can you please explain?"

"Kamal for not formally taking approval from the company before proceeding on leave. And Binoy, in his capacity of being responsible for the batch, not informing his seniors about the non-presence of his colleagues."

Saahas (sarcastically): "But Binoy was not expected to be their leader. So why should he have informed?"

Prashant: "Because he was responsible! And as a leader or a representative, the onus was on him and he was accountable for the batch."

A big silence. Prashant seemed to have lost his temper while Saahas was smiling.

Saahas: "Glad you realized what I was trying to tell from the start."

A bigger silence.

Prashant continued after a minute.

Prashant: "And what else?"

Saahas: "Nothing else. What do you want to hear?"

Prashant: "You missed something."

Saahas: "What?"

Prashant: "What about your last day at CPTI? How did it end?"

Saahas thought for a while and continued.

17

Yudhishthira - 3

31st December was supposed to be our last day in the institute. A Valedictory was organized on the day, followed by High Tea. Being still relatively new to the Corporate Setup, the Valedictory had a lesser meaning for most of us, with a major focus being on the free snacks to be served after the session. Binoy asked Subbu regarding the agenda of the Valedictory. Subbu shared that there will be a few speeches by the Chairman of the institute, Gopal Sir, regarding the 6-month program concluded. Subbu will and the students can share their thoughts if they want to. It was going to be an hour-long program.

For the Valedictory, everyone was dressed up in smart casuals, a combination of collared T-shirts, half-sleeve shirts, and blue and black jeans. I went along with Rohit and Pallavi to the auditorium, and 10 minutes later Binoy and Kamal came in with the rest of the people. After 10 minutes of all of us being seated in the hall, the directors, three of them along with Gopal Sir, the Chairman, entered and sat on the stage, along with Subbu.

The speeches began shortly afterwards, led by Subbu. Subbu gave a short introduction about the course and the progress that the students had made over the last 6 months.

He mentioned the efforts that the institute's staff had put in to make the program a success. While it was supposed to be training for the students, the professors had also learned a lot from the students, especially the need to think on their feet and deliver messages effectively. He said that while he would like to, he could not reveal the instances which provided these learnings. The students smiled and were relieved that Subbu chose not to reveal the instances in front of the Directors and Gopal Sir.

Subbu's speech was long but interesting as all of us went down memory lane of the last 6 months. After his speech, Gopal Sir spoke and shared the importance of discipline and long-term planning to achieve success in careers. While not boring, there wasn't anything new in the speech that the students hadn't heard earlier. Everyone was happy that the speech was short. But the happiness was short-lived as after the speech ended, Subbu asked the students to come up on stage and say something. We were under the impression that only Gopal Sir and Subbu would say something, but it was not to be.

Silence sprang across the hall. During such moments, 5 seconds seem like an eternity. Pallavi took the initiative, not for the first time, and went up the stage. Each one of us thanked her for saving the day. She in turn thanked Subbu for the amazing 6 months at the institute and shared her experiences, including the good times, the learnings gathered, and how she, along with others, was feeling empowered about a successful career forward. She ended by saying that she had started her training with nineteen colleagues; she was now ending with nineteen friends.

After her speech, Subbu asked others to come up on stage but not before he had thanked Pallavi for taking the initiative and teased her by saying, "Never consider your colleagues as your friends." The students smiled while the directors smirked.

Subbu asked others to come on stage. Again, a 5-second silence gave a 1-hour-long feeling. Subbu felt a bit uneasy; we felt very uneasy. Each of us looked at each other's faces. Subbu then shot his key arrow. He asked the representative for the Batch to come on stage and say something. We again looked at each other's faces but with a different tone. I gestured toward Binoy, since he was the current representative, to go on stage. Binoy, in turn, asked me to go ahead, since I had been one.

I decided to walk up.

"Respected Professors, thank you for the amazing last 6 months here at this premier institute of the country. I must, first of all, thank Mr. Suburaj for the amazing support he has provided to all of us and has been like an elder brother, if I can say so, during these 6 months. He has tried to adopt innovative methods of teaching and while we may choose to agree or disagree on the methods, I think we would all agree on the positive intent that Mr. Suburaj has had during these 6 months."

Subbu smiled.

"Over the last months, colleagues, sorry, friends, we have seen good days and not-so-good days and just like we should in real life, we have tried to embrace these with equanimity. Friends, thank you for giving me the opportunity from Day

1, rather Day 2 to be sure, to lead you and I am sure we have also among us seen good days and not-so-good days." All of us laughed.

"Finally, I would like to close by saying that the knowledge that we have gained over the last 6 months should be considered as an asset and a privilege, which we should deploy over the coming six decades and more to create an impact on the power sector and create a better society and a better world. Thank you."

I thanked everyone and was moving away from the dice when Subbu said,

"You, in my opinion, did a good job as a representative. Why don't you share what your experience was in handling the job?" I felt happy at the compliment but nervous about what to say. I could simply recite a small poem 'Winds of Change' which I had thought about 5 months back.

After I finished the poem, there was a 5-second silence in the audience. This time around, this seemed like an hour long to only one person, who was standing on the stage. It was followed by a huge round of applause.

I came down from the stage and sat next to Rohit. He congratulated me on the speech.

Subbu came up to the mic and thanked me for the speech and the poem.

He asked one last time if someone wanted to say something. Binoy went up and shared his experiences. After Binoy's speech, Subbu asked one of the Directors on the stage to give the Vote of Thanks. After the brief Vote of Thanks, Subbu brought the session to a close. Everyone got on the stage for a group photo and then moved to the room adjoining the Hall for tea, coffee, and sandwiches.

Everyone in our batch, including, surprisingly, Binoy and Kamal, came over to congratulate me on the speech.

I, for some reason, could only give a small smile and say thank you. We chatted casually for 15 minutes and started leaving the hall.

As Rohit and I were leaving, Subbu came up to me and asked:

Subbu: "So, how long did it take to write the speech?"

Saahas: "Sir, it was an extempore."

Subbu: "I don't believe it. And what about the poem?"

"Two days to write and five months to think."

Both of us looked at each other. There was silence. That uneasy silence which is a peaceful one.

His eyes conveyed a "Do well, brother." My eyes conveyed a "Thank you for everything." Both of us hugged, and shortly Rohit and I left the hall.

The next day, all of us left the institute. One last time.

18

And it ends?

Prashant: "I have taken around 40 exit interviews, but I am moved by this story."

Saahas: "How many interviews have you said this?" questioned with a slight smirk.

Prashant (with a slightly surprised expression): "Hmm… Okay. On that note, I would like to thank you for your time."

Saahas: "Thank you to you too, for everything."

Prashant and Saahas stood up. They shook hands, and Saahas started moving toward the door.

Saahas was about to open the door when he moved away.

Saahas: "Before I leave, can I ask a question?"

Prashant: "Sure. Please go ahead."

Saahas: "Did I do the right thing?"

Prashant: "You did what you thought was the right thing for everyone, after thinking through the consequences. At times, it is not about what you did, but why you did it. And in my opinion, you did a good job."

Saahas had a smile on his face. After all, even the seemingly toughest folks need some appreciation.

Prashant: "Also, one thing, in fact, that I forgot to ask which you have left blank in your exit form. Where are you headed next?"

Saahas: "What are the options? Another job? MBA? Own startup? Might just. If nothing else, an author most likely."

Prashant: "Do you have a story?"

Saahas: "I might just have had one." Saahas gave a smile.

Prashant: "Good luck. Just remember, being a manager is a chance, being a leader is a choice. And when it is your life, you can be a leader every day, every moment."

Saahas: "Thanks a lot for the advice, Prashant." Saahas said in an assertively proud manner.

Before Saahas could open the door, Prashant's secretary Naina knocked on the door. Prashant asked her to wait if it wasn't urgent.

Naina, however, continued,

"Prashant, I missed sharing the last page of the printout you asked me to give before this meeting. Came to hand this over. Really sorry for this."

"It's okay Naina. Thank you," Prashant said.

Prashant read the page which had only one question and a slightly long answer.

Prashant looked at Saahas with a warm smile,

Saahas (exasperated expression, wondering what was next but not showing in his words): "What now, Prashant?"

"You are indeed more than just a name, Saahas. Thank you." Prashant said.

"Thank you too."

With that, Saahas left the room. Prashant also left after Saahas.

* * *

The noise from the air conditioner coming through the vent regained its role to disturb the uneasy peace in the room. The papers were left on the table.

One paper with a single question and a slightly long answer was set aside. It read,

'Question:

How would you describe your role as the representative?

Answer:

When blow the winds of change,

And you have got no one else to blame.

When in the journey of life, you have to make a call,

And you know not whether to run away, or give it your all.

When circumstances are big, you small,

And you have got no support to fall.

When the road ahead is too long,

And you can be anything but wrong.

When situations are there for you to tame,

And it all becomes more than just a game.

When every moment is a challenge new,

And for trying out, the options are few.

You have to realize that no two worlds are the same,

And prove that you are more than just a name!

* * *

* 9 7 9 8 8 9 6 7 3 3 6 7 6 *